Eastern Chipmunks

Secrets of Their Solitary Lives

TEXT AND PHOTOGRAPHS BY LAWRENCE WISHNER

Smithsonian Institution Press, Washington, D.C.

© 1982 by Smithsonian Institution. All rights reserved.
Printed in the United States of America
First edition

Library of Congress Cataloging in Publication Data
Wishner, Lawrence Arndt.
Eastern chipmunks.
(A Smithsonian nature book)
Bibliography: p.
Includes index.
1. Eastern chipmunk.   I. Title.   II. Series.
QL737.R68W53   599.32'32   82-860
ISBN 0-87474-962-X   AACR2

The paper in this book meets the guidelines for permanence
and durability of the Committee on Production Guidelines
for Book Longevity of the Council on Library Resources.

Frontispiece   Gutrune's youngsters at play.

Dedicated to

Samuel and Shirley Wishner

Nancy and Catherine Wishner

Lady Cheltenham and her companions

Contents

Preface

This book is about chipmunks. In particular, it is about Eastern chipmunks (*Tamias striatus*) that inhabit, as you might have suspected, the eastern half of the United States and Canada. Even more specifically, it deals with the race of chipmunks (*Tamias striatus fisheri*) that lives on the East Coast of the United States between southern New York in the north, Virginia in the south, and eastern Ohio in the west. It attempts to address every accessible aspect of their lives.

Their behavior and life history are compared with published reports concerning those of other races living in other parts of the range, but primarily the book describes the fifty-nine resident and forty-nine transient chipmunks studied on 1.5 acres of land located in Spotsylvania County, Virginia, over a six-year period between 1974 and 1980. The study area is located at an elevation of 250 feet in the Piedmont province of Virginia, three miles west of the city of Fredericksburg and the Fall Line (38°18′00″N, 77°31′40″W), and is an oak-hickory forest edge interspersed with dogwood, tupelo, and American holly. It is bounded on the east by an intermittent stream, on the south by an open lawn, on the west by state road 694, and on the north by open fields. Slightly to the west of the center sits a stone house surrounded by about thirty feet of unkept lawn. It is nearly ideal chipmunk habitat, teeming with seemingly happy chipmunks.

The study's principal technique has been direct observation, frequently enhanced by the use of seven- or ten-power field glasses, and supplemented with still photography, sound recording, and comparisons with the literature. It cannot be overemphasized that the uniqueness of this study lies in its continuous day-to-day observation of 108 individual chipmunks for a period of six years. During those six years some of the subjects were born, some died, some lived out their entire lives. This book is a tribute to their cooperation in revealing their family histories and relationships, their adventures and romances, and their private lives in general.

The book is structured as a chronological narrative into which are woven the details and conclusions concerning the chipmunk's life history. The result is the illumination of the nature of this small animal, whose presence and activity in the rural and suburban areas of eastern North America are a delight to both nature enthusiasts and casual wildlife observers, but are not completely understood. Chapter 9 consists of a brief summary of the chipmunk's life history and habits, to which the reader may wish to refer frequently or occasionally, or may even wish to read thoroughly before beginning the other chapters.

All sources consulted in the writing of this book are listed in the Bibliography. Specific references are cited in the Notes.

For their assistance and encouragement throughout the study and the preparation of the manuscript, I am indebted to more people than I could ever acknowledge, but particularly to Dr. Richard Thorington and Dr. Michael Carleton of the National Museum of Natural History; Sheila McGarr of the Mary Washington College Library; Jack Marquardt of the NMNH Library; Dr. Michael Bass of the Mary Washington College Biology Department, who graciously allowed me to try out most of this material on his ecology classes; and Janet Fraser of the Mary Washington College Philosophy Department, who provided me with philosophical insights into the mind of the chipmunk. In particular, I must thank Dr. Thorington and Dr. Robert Emry for allowing me access to some of their material on the phylogeny of the squirrels prior to its publication. Finally, I am deeply grateful to Ted Rivinus and Maureen Jacoby of the Smithsonian Institution Press for their patience and encouragement and especially to Hope Pantell for her editing skills and insights.

Figure 1. A chipmunk named Pickwick shows off his impeccable striped cloak.

1

Little Chipmunk, Who Are You?

Little animal, who are you?
I am Chipmunk!
I am what you see,
She said with a wink;
I am what I do,
Not what you think;
If you wish to know me,
My song is yours too.

Whether or not man is an endangered species may be a favorite topic for discussion when chipmunks get together—but not too close together—to sing on an April morning. If we do not do likewise, it is for the obvious reason that chipmunks are far from endangered.

Chipmunks have learned to live in close contact with man, but nevertheless independently of man. They do not become dependent and, perhaps, that is the very heart of their charm. Their cousins, the tree squirrels, do become dependent. They overpopulate suburban areas, become sneaky, comical, and ungainly as they depend more and more on man's conscious or unconscious unselfishness. Chipmunks, in their independence, always retain what naturalist John Burroughs called their sylvan airiness and delicacy, their nervous restlessness, wild beauty, jauntiness, archness, and suspicion. Of course, chipmunks know nothing of this.

The Eastern chipmunk, *Tamias striatus,* is a small diurnal rodent of the Sciuridae, or squirrel, family. The term diurnal refers to its daylight activity, as opposed to nocturnal animals, which are active at night, and crepuscular animals, which are active during twilight. For those who admire the scientist's precision, the taxonomic history and descriptions of the genus *Tamias* and the subspecies *Tamias striatus fisheri,* the race that inhabits Virginia, are given in Appendixes C and D.

The chipmunk wears a characteristically striped cloak (fig. 1), lives in an underground burrow, but travels on the surface and into the trees. Among its varied behavioral repertoire, three characteristics stand out:

1. The ability to engage in short-term hibernation.
2. An intense food-hoarding instinct.
3. Solitary behavior and extreme independence.

It will be seen that the first two of these are responsible for the third.

The chipmunk's activity on three levels—fossorial (underground), terrestrial (on the surface), and arboreal (in the trees)—allows it extreme versatility and independence. Its fossorial home and ability to hibernate for short periods allow the chipmunk to retire from the rigors of bad weather. But probably most important, the chipmunk, while tolerating man's intrusion into its habitat, has maintained its independence through opportunism and hard work. While tree squirrels are known to become dependent on the food supplied by their human benefactors, the chipmunk fills its capacious cheek pouches to bulging capacity (fig. 2) over and over, day after day, during every season of its activity, and carries food home to its underground burrow in response to what appears to the observer to be an obsessive genetic fear of starvation. When food is scarce, it has its stored supply. When food is plentiful, it becomes more active in obtaining the greater share of the wealth. This cushion of food, upon which the chipmunk literally sleeps, allows it to maintain its aloofness. Thus, the chipmunk is introduced to us as the living example of thrift, industry, charm, and independence, although, it must be repeated, it knows nothing of these human attributes.

I seriously doubt that anyone who knows them, no matter how obscurely, would deny chipmunks a favored place among woodland creatures in their hearts. The

Figure 2. Lady Cheltenham, the heroine of this book, demonstrates the capacious nature of her cheek pouches by carrying six acorns.

general lack of understanding and knowledge concerning their admittedly secretive lives might, then, seem to be a mystery. The fact is, however, that, in spite of their delightful antics that make the woods come alive, they are of no commercial value or significance. Consequently, few professional naturalists have been able to earn a living revealing the secrets of their solitary lives. Although some European courtiers in past centuries may have engaged in the thoroughly disgusting practice of lining their capes with Siberian chipmunk pelts for their unique and fashionable appearance, this reprehensible behavior has been abandoned, principally because the pelts were not very warm.

On the other side of the ledger, the Eastern chipmunk has yet to be convicted by any but the most circumstantial evidence of being a pest to farmers, gardeners, housewives, or anyone else. In our society, a delightful, fascinating, and unsubversive creature that minds its own business, is simply not spied upon. Our excuse, then, for invading the chipmunks' privacy is to discover what makes them so delightful and fascinating, that is to say, what makes them so independent and what makes their independence of value. The chipmunk is an ideal subject for a study of this type because it is available and convenient and it tends to resist human influence strongly.

From a purely intellectual point of view the Eastern chipmunk is fascinating because *Tamias* is evolutionarily and behaviorally one of the most primitive genera of living squirrels as well as one of the most solitary mammals. Craig Black proposed a phylogenetic, or family, tree for the North American squirrels based upon the existence of *Tamias*, an ancestor of the Eastern chipmunk, in fossil deposits dating back to the early Miocene epoch 25 million years ago. In his proposal, *Tamias* formed the trunk of the tree. Squirrels appear to have come into their own during the early Oligocene, almost 40 million years ago. They also seem, from the locations of

the fossil deposits, to have been forest-dwelling, semiarboreal, seed, nut, and berry eaters just like the Eastern chipmunk today.

During the period from the mid-Oligocene through the Miocene, the elevation of the Rocky Mountains resulted in a decrease in precipitation in the great Plains, which in turn caused forest-bounding streams and lakes, as well as the scrub forest and grasslands remote from water, to change to more open plains and grassland. During the early Pliocene, the elevation of the Cascades and the Sierra Nevada produced a similar change in the Great Basin leading from forest to grassland and, in some areas, desert. Whatever squirrels may have been present before these events took place, it is not difficult to imagine how the Eastern chipmunk's ancestor, with its ability to live under, on, or above the ground, would have been able to adapt throughout the next 10 million years or so and eventually give rise to the present forms.

More recent evidence has, however, denied *Tamias* its status as the trunk of the family tree by showing that the Oligocene squirrels probably more closely resembled tree squirrels. The differentiation of the ground squirrel lineage, *Tamias* and two extinct genera (*Miospermophilus* and *Protospermophilus*), from *Protosciurus*, the extinct arboreal ancestor of all of the squirrels, appears to have taken place during the early Oligocene. Figure 3 is a simplified representation of this family tree. Based upon the importance of the Eastern chipmunk's ancestor, the logical sequence of events, as outlined in the previous paragraphs, shows how speculative geologic explanations of evolutionary events can be. The newer interpretation is based primarily on the discovery by Robert J. Emry and Richard W. Thorington, Jr., of a nearly complete skeleton of *Protosciurus* from the early Oligocene, a skeleton closely resembling that of the modern fox

squirrel. We chipmunk enthusiasts can only hope that some day an even older chipmunk skeleton will come to light.

Let us examine the placement of the recent squirrels on this tree and compare it with the behavioral summary given in figure 4. The arrangements in these figures are not meant to imply the superiority or inferiority of any particular adaptation, but merely to show a transition from fossorial to arboreal behavior. Beginning on the right of the family tree, the marmots, represented by the ground hog or woodchuck in the eastern United States, are fossorial, spending most of their time underground, are frequently solitary, and store body fat rather than food during the summer so that they can hibernate deeply for three months

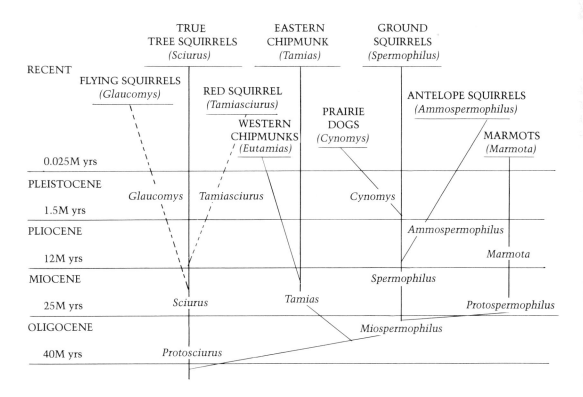

Figure 3. A simplified family tree of the North American squirrels. Where known, the first appearance of both living and extinct forms is shown by their lowest position here. Broken lines indicate probable relationships.

Figure 4. Comparison of habits of different members of the squirrel family.

	Primary Body Form	Nest	Major Activity	Winter Inactivity?	Stores Food?	Solitary?
Marmots	Digging	Burrow	Ground	Hibernates	No	Yes**
Ground squirrels	Digging	Burrow	Ground	Maybe (Most)	Some	Yes*
Antelope squirrels	Digging/ scampering	Burrow	Ground	Maybe	Some	Yes
Prairie dogs	Digging	Burrow	Ground	Maybe (Most)	Some	Colonial
Eastern chipmunks	Scampering	Burrow	Ground/trees	Maybe	Yes	Yes
Western chipmunks	Scampering	Burrow	Ground/trees	Maybe	Yes	Yes
Red squirrels	Climbing	Trees	Trees/ground	No	Yes	No
True tree squirrels	Climbing	Trees	Trees	No	Some	No
Flying squirrels	Climbing	Trees	Trees	No	Some	No

*Some species gregarious   **Some species colonial

or more during the winter. Their body form is adapted for digging. Moving to the left, the ground squirrels and antelope squirrels of the western United States hibernate where the climate demands it, but are much more mobile than the marmots. The prairie dogs do not hibernate deeply or generally and their elaborate burrow existence classifies them as quite fossorial. Western chipmunks behave similarly to their eastern cousins, except that they move faster and are therefore better adapted to life in more open country.

The red squirrels are arboreal, spending much of their time in the trees (although they are on the ground more than other tree squirrels). They do not store food centrally like chipmunks and do not hibernate at all. Their body form is adapted for climbing. The true tree squirrels are more distinctly arboreal, spend little time on the ground, store food inefficiently, and are active all winter. The flying squirrels, which actually glide rather than fly, are superbly adapted to arboreal existence when the trees are far apart. All three of the tree squirrels are much more gregarious than most of the ground and burrowing

squirrels, huddling together in nests to keep warm during the winter. The colonial behavior of the prairie dogs and several species of marmots is probably a response to climate and to their relationships with predators. All of this leaves the Eastern chipmunk in the middle, adapted to all three levels of existence like his Miocene ancestor.

After the change from forest to grassland in the West, it was logical for the Eastern chipmunk to remain in the ancient forests of the East and for the Western chipmunks to remain in the more open spaces. The original wide range of both is supported by the presence of *Eutamias* fossils in late glacial deposits in Virginia and *Tamias* fossils in deposits of similar age in Texas, areas where they do not exist today. Although Black suggested from the fossil record that the Western chipmunks diverged from the Eastern chipmunks during the early Pleistocene, L. Scott Ellis and Linda R. Maxson, using an immunological technique, suggested that the two genera were distinct as early as the late Miocene.

Is it possible that the Eastern chipmunk has survived and prospered for almost 25 million years simply by minding its own business? Does the Eastern chipmunk's similarity to its Miocene ancestor imply that its behavior is primitive when compared with that of the other squirrels? As we shall see, there are aspects of its behavior—most of them derived from its solitary nature—that we might be tempted to call primitive. If indeed its behavior seems primitive when compared with human behavior, we must remember that the test of evolutionary success and advancement is the survival and prosperity of the individual, its relatives, and its descendants. No one can doubt that chipmunks have survived and prospered. They must have something going for them. What seems primitive from our point of view cannot be all bad. By not tolerating each other, they avoid the problem of putting up with their in-laws!

In summary, the chipmunk is far less an endangered species than the human. This delightful animal, which turns its back on us even as it eats out of our hand, has been unjustly neglected in prose and verse by that obscure and somewhat strange primate known as *Homo sapiens.* Let us not waste another minute before delivering some of this overdue justice, at least in prose.

2

Lady Cheltenham and Guilford

Chipmunks are wonderful landlords. Although for hundreds, thousands, perhaps millions of years they have owned, by right of possession, the one-and-one-half acres that I now call the Cheltenham Chipmunk Refuge, they have never, in the ten years of my residence, asked that rent be paid. Nor have they proffered a single gesture of gratitude for the 762 pounds of sunflower seeds with which I have supplied them over the past six years in partial compensation for their indifferent cooperation in revealing their secret lives. Their unassuming tolerance has gained my eternal respect and admiration.

I know they have always been here. My first, vague awareness of their presence had occasionally been confirmed by the flash of stripes darting between the woods and the back of the house during the summer, and by the frantic dash of four or five sets of stripes in tandem through the bare woods in late February before they settled down to their solitary and surreptitious existence for another season. Even before my particular interest developed, they had added a dimension to what makes country living a kind of miracle.

Winter seemed to arrive suddenly in 1974. I had spent the leisure hours of the summer and autumn photographing the seasonal succession of toadstools and wildflowers and then suddenly, in late October, my subjects were gone and the cameras became idle. The next weekend a friend brought me a load of firewood and we carefully stacked it on the back porch. We chatted briefly in the driveway and when I returned to the porch, two chipmunks were at work exploring the woodpile like children in a newly discovered playground. The opportunity to photograph them was irresistible.

Since the porch is protected, only thirty feet from the woods, and is accessible from the house through three windows and a door, I soon had electronic lights mounted over the woodpile and a camera focused through one of the windows. In order to simplify exposure calculations, I placed two upturned logs in front of the woodpile, at precalculated exposure distances from the lights, and on these logs I placed what seemed the most logical bait at hand— peanut butter.

At first I thought the whole setup was too simple and too quickly devised to be successful, and I was right. The problem, however, was not with the equipment, but with the bait. Lesson number one: Unlike children, these chipmunks did not eat peanut butter. Realizing subconsciously that I had a lot to learn about chipmunks, I switched to shelled pecans, and soon Lady Cheltenham and Guilford, my first subjects, were performing like veteran models. It occurred to me much later that the chipmunks' dislike for peanut butter may explain why the literature sometimes reports the apparent absence of these animals in areas where one would normally expect them to be found. The survey traps are usually baited with a mixture of peanut butter and rolled oats.

At the outset, I exposed film whenever one of the chipmunks was before the camera, thinking that each appearance was the chance of a lifetime. It was some time before I realized that they were not disturbed by the lights and would return again and again to display their behavioral repertoire in great detail. I finally became more discriminating and waited for the poses and situations that assured good photographs as well as a complete record of their habits.

At this point I should confess that lesson number two was learned less swiftly than lesson number one. Originally, Lady Cheltenham and Guilford had been named Cheltenham and Gutrune (the full names were Cheltenham Rosyrump and Gutrune

Figures 5 and 6. Lady Cheltenham (left) and Guilford. In these typical poses, she impersonates a duckpin and he feigns piety.

von Chip), and it was some time before I realized how carefully the sexes must be examined at this time of year. Not until "Gutrune" emerged from hibernation the following January did my chagrin become inevitable—and his name was changed to Guilford. (The name Gutrune was used again later for another female.) The prefix "Lady" was added to Cheltenham because of the difference in their appearances: her sex was confirmed in action two weeks later. Let us say simply that during November, male and female chipmunks are distinguishable only upon close examination. Brief biographies of Lady Cheltenham and Guilford, along with those of three other chipmunks who have prominent roles in this study, are presented in Appendix A, page 126. A list of all the chipmunks, along with a map of their burrows, is on page 30.

It was evident from the outset that Lady Cheltenham and Guilford did not suffer one another graciously. She appeared to have been born in the spring of 1974; he was probably one season older. Despite his greater size and experience, she found no difficulty in dominating him completely and took control of the back-porch feeding area at once. So complete was her authority that by late November he would not even approach the porch when she was present. During the winter Lady Cheltenham spent many hours in the vacation home we had constructed for her in the woodpile, and my

first and lasting impression was of her independence and self-confidence.

My memory went back to childhood experiences with chipmunks in the Pocono mountains of Pennsylvania, when I was too young and preoccupied to enjoy a systematic curiosity about their lives. But realizing that in order to make good animal photographs one has to know the animals, I consulted some of the standard field guides and learned, for example, that chipmunks could be expected to be seen storing nuts in their underground burrows during the fall of the year, just as they seemed to be doing then.

The white oak acorn crop in 1974 had been the best in years and the ground was covered with the ¾-inch sweet acorns. Lady Cheltenham and Guilford were systematically correcting the situation underfoot by transporting these acorns to their burrows with amazing speed and efficiency. Guilford's front door was in the base of a rotten stump at the edge of the woods about thirty feet east of the house and Lady Cheltenham's was located about forty-five feet northeast—and about forty-five feet north of Guilford's. Hers was simply a two-inch hole in the ground under the leaves. Both homes could be observed from inside the house, and field glasses brought them almost within touching distance. The nature and construction of these burrows are dealt with in chapter 9.

Colorplates 1, 2, and 3. The bulk of a chipmunk's diet consists of nuts, seeds, and fruits with supplements of animal matter, especially for pregnant and lactating mothers and their growing youngsters. One of Guinevere's offspring discovers a pecan (above), while one of Lady Cheltenham's children devours an earthworm in spite of the fact that it is good for him (opposite, top), and another juvenile courts a tummyache by sampling an unripe holly berry (opposite, bottom).

Figures 7 and 8. Gutrune with thirty-five sunflower seeds stuffed into her bulging cheek pouches. In another pose, she devours a maple samara.

The chipmunks were carrying the acorns, six at a time, in their internal cheek pouches. One day in November I watched Lady Cheltenham from her first appearance outside her burrow at dawn to her retirement at dusk. She transported acorns from the opposite side of the house continuously. The round-trip journey of about 200 feet required two minutes, including the time taken to fill her pouches with five acorns (three in one side, two in the other) and pick up the sixth in her mouth. Had she pouched the sixth, she would have been able neither to close her mouth nor fit through her front door. She emerged about 6:00 a.m., breakfasted, harvested between 7:00 a.m. and 12:00 noon in this manner, enjoyed a siesta from 12:00 to 3:00 p.m., and then returned to work until 6:00 p.m., after which she relaxed near her burrow until retiring at dusk. During the periods of intense activity, she rested and groomed herself for about five minutes every four or five trips.

From these observations we can estimate that she carried about 116 acorns per hour and 928 during the day's activity. It was no longer a mystery why the lawn was being cleared so rapidly. Later experiments on pouch capacity showed that Lady Chelten-

ham could carry an average of twelve to fifteen ½-inch willow oak acorns. Gutrune, a female who appeared the following spring and assumed the discarded name, was able to carry an average of thirty-five whole sunflower seeds at a time.

One of the reasons for the chipmunks' independence must be evident now. They certainly do not plan to go hungry. In his beautiful essay on the chipmunk in *Under the Apple-Trees,* John Burroughs described how his Catskill chipmunk carried home five quarts of hickory nuts and one quart of chestnuts during a three-day period. Lang Elliott, in his remarkable study of Adirondack chipmunks, excavated several burrows during the spring, collected the stored food, and calculated, from its reported energy content and the energy requirements of an average chipmunk; the time period during which a chipmunk could live on it. In one case, to both his and my amazement, he found a male chipmunk with an eleven-month food supply that remained from the previous year's harvest even after the owner had lived on it over the winter!

There can be no doubt that chipmunks do not store food to satisfy their immediate needs, but rather because they are genetically programmed to do so, and that this instinctive characteristic has enabled them to remain independent for 25 million or so years. It may have enabled them to remain happy as well.

The provisions stored by chipmunks are strictly nonperishable. Natural nuts in Virginia include acorns, pecans, hickory nuts, beech nuts, and horse chestnuts, all unshelled. I have further tempted them with walnuts, Brazil nuts, almonds, fresh peanuts, and Ohio buckeyes. It is curious how they take so readily to Brazil nuts and peanuts, which neither they nor their local ancestors have ever seen. Roasted peanuts are avoided like peanut butter. Among natural seeds are sunflower, corn, maple samaras, and wild cherry stones (after they have eaten the cherries). Less popular are whole wheat, dried peas, soybeans, and pumpkin seeds. How chipmunks know not to store perishable foods was explained by Burroughs:

> He did know it, but not as you and I know it, by experience; he knew it as all the wild creatures know how to get on in the world, by the wisdom that pervades nature, and is much older than we or they are.

Carrying this to the extreme, chipmunks even seem to be able to detect and avoid acorns that contain weevil eggs. During the fall of 1975 my daughter and I collected a variety of acorns from a wide area in order to determine whether or not chipmunks had a preference for white oak (sweet) acorns or black oak (bitter) acorns. When we placed these on the porch we noticed that some were not taken, including those that showed the small holes through which the hatched weevils had already escaped. A weevil eventually emerged from each of the other avoided acorns. Although Elliott reported finding weevil-infested beech nuts in the burrows of his Adirondack chipmunks, Virginia chipmunks seem to be more discriminating, perhaps because they have a greater bounty and a wider choice because of the longer summer season. They, incidentally, showed no preference between the sweet or bitter acorns, but took the larger ones of either variety first.

The large caches found in burrows are better understood when we realize that, contrary to the reports in some field guides, chipmunks store food not only in the fall but throughout the season, and make very efficient use of their food supply. The storage of cherry stones after the fruit has been eaten is a good example. The preferential location of the burrows at the forest edge allows chipmunks to take advantage of the harvest of nuts from the trees as well as the seeds and fruits from open land, while the trees provide cover from avian predators. Capable climbers, chipmunks harvest beech and hickory nuts from the tree tops as well as from the ground.

The literature contains many reports of chipmunks caching provisions in locations other than the burrows (scatter-hoarding). There are only two situations under which I have observed this phenomenon. Young chipmunks who have not yet established a burrow hide food wherever they feel it will be secure, in response to their hoarding instinct, then frequently neglect to return to it. Females, after weaning their young in the burrow, remain afield for long periods of time, during which they may scatter-hoard in order to avoid returning to the burrow and the demands of their milk-hungry children. When they are ready to reenter the burrow, they usually gather the scattered hoards and take them home.

In addition to hoarded foods, which are used during the winter and for weaning the young, the chipmunk's diet is quite rich and not at all fastidious. Although nuts, seeds, and fruits make up the bulk of the diet, mushrooms and animal matter are also important. Earthworms, slugs, grubs, and various insects are popular, especially with young, growing chipmunks and females carrying young or in lactation. Frogs and salamanders have been reported in their diet, and one of the vilest of sights must be that of a chipmunk peeling a prickly caterpillar like a banana while consuming the green innards.

Colorplate 4. Guinevere's youngster explores the home range. After the first day or two following emergence—about six weeks after birth—young chipmunks venture away from the security of the burrow entrance and scale the castle walls while safely blending into their environment.

Colorplate 5. Family portrait on emergence day: Lady Cheltenham poses with five of her six children, crowded around the burrow entrance. The sixth youngster is not seen because a sibling's feet are planted on its head in the burrow.

Colorplate 6. Maternal care is tender and discipline is sometimes stern. Lady Cheltenham firmly escorts a youngster home after it seemed to wander too far into its undiscovered world.

During the summer of 1979, Virginia was subjected to the howl of the 17-year-cicadas. The sight of happy chipmunks gorging gluttonously on succulent cicadas was truly heartwarming! Literature reports of chipmunks eating the brains of baby birds have not been substantiated here. Perhaps Virginia chipmunks are more gentle than others. On one occasion I was fascinated to watch Mistress Appleford deftly catch a field mouse and take it home to her recently weaned youngsters. By another account Virginia chipmunks may be less discriminating than others. Bridget and Heinz Henisch, in their delightful *Chipmunk Portrait,* refer to ants as the chipmunk's caviar. Virginia chipmunks do not seem to be as aristocratic as their Pennsylvania cousins; I have never seen them show the least interest in ants.

Among the fruits favored in this area are wild cherries, dewberries, grapes, holly berries, pipsissewa berries, nandina berries, and dogwood berries. Chipmunks have succumbed to the temptation of offered strawberries, apples, peaches, and plums, but not pineapple or citrus fruits. Banana is a favorite.

A final word on the chipmunk's diet must speak to the popular belief among gardeners that the poor maligned animals dig up and eat bulbs. Although this is almost universally believed, the evidence is strictly circumstantial, of the hearsay variety. With the exception of several descriptions of the importance of the bulb of the wild trout lily to the diet of northern chipmunks, I have been unable to locate a single person who has actually seen a chipmunk perform such a dastardly deed in anyone's garden. As a simple test, I left a box of roots and bulbs, given to me when my mother left Virginia, on the back-porch woodpile for an entire season. The bulbs and roots of iris, day lilies, various daffodils, crocuses, tulips, and amaryllis were carefully counted and remained intact for the entire season despite the exploratory presence in the box of at least thirty different chipmunks on many occasions.

There were in the box other types of bulbs that I was supposed to plant in order to find out what they were. Since I didn't, I can't identify them, but they also remained unmolested.

In conjunction with diet, the water requirements of the chipmunk should be mentioned, especially since much of their diet comprises seeds and nuts, which contain little water. In spite of this, the requirement for external water is difficult to demonstrate. Joseph A. Panuska and Nelson J. Wade have reported laboratory captive chipmunks drinking about one ounce per day when fed dry commercial rations. Although chipmunks drink readily from the water dish on the porch, if I forget to fill it, they ignore it totally and do not even investigate to see if it contains water.

During the summer of 1976, Gutrune remained in her burrow for three weeks, retiring one week before the birth of her young and just as she was coming into lactation. She bore a litter of six and during the first two weeks of lactation must have produced more than a quart of milk, which is about 87 percent water. Where did she obtain the water? Excavated burrows have sometimes contained ground water in their lowest tunnels and even may contain drainage tunnels, but Gutrune's burrow was next to the well in which the water level is thirty feet below the surface. As we shall see later, Gutrune was a champion burrower, but thirty feet of vertical digging was beyond even her capacity. The obvious explanation is metabolic water, which is water produced during the energy metabolism of nutrients and on which the antelope squirrels seem to be able to survive indefinitely, but the quantity involved is hard to swallow (no pun intended). During life on the surface, a combination of condensation, metabolic water, and succulent foods certainly produces sufficient water for survival in dry weather.

The varying food supply throughout the season requires the chipmunk to move about in different areas at different times. Consequently, it is difficult to define its

home range, or the total land area in which it exists during its life, even though that home range is necessarily small. It is small because the chipmunk is small and because it lives in a permanent burrow to which it must return frequently.

In the past, the home ranges of small animals have been determined by system-atic live-trapping. Ralph W. Yerger summarized a number of these studies when he suggested that the average home range of an adult male chipmunk was about 1/3 acre, about 1/4 acre for an average adult female, and 1/5 acre for an average juvenile. One of the problems with many older studies has been that the range was not

Colorplate 7. A young chipmunk's curiosity knows no bounds. Gutrune's child demurely admires a flower during its first explorations of its new world outside the burrow.

Colorplate 8. After a few days of exploring nature, young chipmunks turn to the discovery of themselves as mirrored by their siblings. In a week or so they will settle into their solitary adult lives and approach one another only with aggression. Here, two of Gutrune's youngsters appear to be kissing, but undertones of aggressiveness are already present. A third youngster watches from the burrow. (See also frontispiece.)

necessarily examined over an entire season to reflect changes that result from varying population activity and availability of food. The area within which a chipmunk lives today or this week, in July for example, may be entirely different from the area in which it will harvest wild cherries in August, or acorns in October.

When a female has young in the burrow, she will stay closer to home, and when a male is searching for eligible females during a mating season, he may travel great distances from home. As a result, the home range must be examined over at least an entire season, and preferably over several seasons, in order to reflect yearly changes in the patterns of food availability. Some foods may not be available every year.

Using visual observation, Elliott found the home ranges of Adirondack chipmunks to be quite a bit larger than previously thought, but presented them only for particular times of the year. The home ranges of four chipmunks in this study, based upon continuous observation and the connection of points beyond which they were never seen to travel during at least three seasons, are shown in figure 11, which is a map of the Cheltenham Chipmunk Refuge. Lady Cheltenham (burrow no. 1) remained within 0.49 acre, both Gutrune (burrow no. 2) and Mistress Earwicker (burrow no. 23) remained within 0.46 acre, and Fenwick (burrows no. 3 and 3a), the only male I was able to keep such close track of, remained within 0.98 acre. Fenwick's double-sized area reflects his eagerness to pursue the ladies during the mating seasons. Although not measured precisely, the home ranges of the others were similar.

It seems a reasonable assumption, and is supported by observation in homogeneous areas, that is, large areas of consistent topography, that a chipmunk's burrow will be in the approximate center of its home range. Figure 11 shows that this is not necessarily the case. The reason for this discrepancy is that the area is *not* homogeneous. It is bounded on the north by an open field, on the east by an intermittent stream, and on the south by an open lawn. All of these are natural barriers to free movement and tend to cause lopsided home ranges when the burrow is close to a boundary. Areas of seasonal foraging are frequently found at the edge of the home range.

Another interesting feature of the chipmunk's home range is that it overlaps the home ranges of other chipmunks and its size is not severely regulated by population density. One might ask why a chipmunk, which obviously does not suffer other chipmunks gladly, does not defend its home range from intruders; that is, why it is not conspicuously territorial like the red squirrel. Actually, chipmunks are territorial to the extent that they will defend a small area of about seventy-five square feet surrounding their burrows, an area from which they can always be counted on to chase other chipmunks if aware of their presence. This is sometimes referred to as a "core area," but satisfies the definition of a territory given by William H. Burt in his Michigan study. More will be said about territoriality when we take up social behavior in chapter 6. In any event, chipmunks do not defend their entire home ranges from intruders as red squirrels do.

Theoretical reasons for this have been proposed, but I think the simplest answer lies in the fact that, unlike the red squirrel, which spends most of its time in trees, where it can observe most of its home range, the chipmunk spends most of its time on the ground, where visibility is limited, and underground, where visibility is nonexistent. Every courageous chipmunk knows that if it wanders into the home range, or even the territory, of another chipmunk, the likelihood is that the resident will either be in another part of its or another's home range or incommunicado in its burrow. Consequently, territoriality cannot always be asserted and home ranges may overlap. The larger home range of the red squirrel is also more likely to be homogeneous.

The chipmunk's foraging behavior within its home range has been illuminated on the basis of the "Central Place Foraging Theory," a theoretical principle that can be simply stated as opportunism. When foraging chipmunks find a quantity of food, they promptly take it home and if they are not able to carry all of it at once, they return as many times as required before continuing to forage. To expect a chipmunk to survey several feeding opportunities and then, either consciously or instinctively, choose the best one is contrary to the animal's independent and opportunistic nature. Furthermore, in view of the excessive quantities of food hoarded, it is not necessary or even of advantage to its survival.

In November 1974 Lady Cheltenham and Guilford were foraging their opportunistic little hearts out at a rate of 116 acorns per hour in preparation for a winter that, for Lady Cheltenham, was mostly business as usual. As they dashed about "with the usual calamitous air," as Annie Dillard puts it in *Pilgrim at Tinker Creek*, they demonstrated their unique and endearing manner of travel. It is not easy, I suspect, for anything as small as a chipmunk to find its way around a big world with its eyes only an inch or two from the ground. Each bush is a giant tree and each blade of grass must be like a parking meter. I have tried, to the consternation of my neighbors, to obtain their perspective on the world, but my chin keeps getting in the way and all I see is the ground. Some day I will dig a hole and look at the forest over the edge of it.

Both Lady Cheltenham and Guilford moved about their home ranges with a freedom and confidence that comes from familiarity, but they seemed to follow well-learned routes that led from one landmark to another. These landmarks were bushes, trees, and other objects that possessed elevation and could be seen from a distance.

Their movements were always characteristic: a mad dash of ten or twelve feet, an alert pause with their eyes and ears sensitive to all around them, then another mad dash, and so forth, frequently pausing to take advantage of the elevation of a log, a stump, a low branch, or the trunk of a tree. When crossing open areas, the mad dash is usually long enough to reach cover, and if something upsets them before the halfway point, they return to their last stopping place. If alerted after the halfway point, their speed accelerates to the next stopping place. Their alertness and suspicion are certainly unique among animals. John Burroughs summarized it beautifully:

> I would not say he is burdened with a conscious sense of danger; rather is his fear instinctive and unconscious. It is in his blood—born with him and part of his life.
>
> He is on the lookout for danger as constantly as he is on the lookout for food, and takes no more thought about the one than about the other. His heart beats as fast as the ticking of a watch, and all his movements are as abrupt and spasmodic as if they were born of alarm.

The intensity of the chipmunks' hoarding instinct, which the less enlightened might refer to as greed, is the only force that seems to dominate their caution. I have noticed that they will routinely allow me to approach much more closely than usual when they are taking provisions from a well-stocked feeding site. Although I have lost the source, a story is told of a chipmunk familiar with live traps that burrowed under one and removed most of the bait through the wire-mesh bottom, but so intense was its hoarding instinct, that it then entered the trap and was caught while removing the last few kernels of corn.

The end of the fall season of 1974 was not as abrupt as its beginning. The reason was that Lady Cheltenham, as is frequently the case during a chipmunk's first season, carried on business as usual over most of the winter. Guilford, on the other hand, became lazy during the last week in November, ceased collecting the many acorns still available, sat around gazing pensively at the leaf-abandoned woods, and

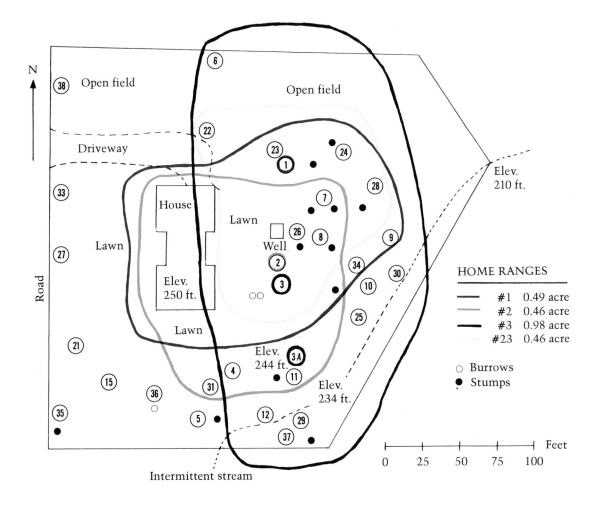

Burrow No.	Residents	Dates of Residence
1.	Lady Cheltenham	Fall 1974 – March 1979
	Mistress Earwicker	May 1979 – July 1979
	Clorindas	Summer 1979 – present
2.	Guilford	Fall 1974 – March 1975
	Gutrune	March 1975 – August 1977
3.	Fenwick	Spring 1975 – Fall 1976
3a.	Fenwick	Fall 1976 – Summer 1979
4.	Diarmuid	Summer 1975 – Summer 1976
	Don Diego	Summer 1976 – Fall 1977
	Dorcas	Summer 1978
	Dierdre	Spring 1979 – present
5.	Hannibal	Spring 1975 – Summer 1976
	Zerlina	Spring 1978
	Petruchio	Summer 1980 – present
6.	Pickwick	Summer 1975 – Spring 1976
	Rinaldo	Summer 1976 – Spring 1977
7.	Launcelot	Spring 1976 – March 1977
	Rinaldo	March 1977 – Winter 1977
	Willoughby	March 1978 – Winter 1978
	Rosalinda	Summer 1980 – present

Figure 11. Map of the Cheltenham Chipmunk Refuge. Burrow residents, from the fall of 1974 to the present, are listed below.

8.	Guinevere	Fall 1975 – Summer 1979
9.	Ringtail	Summer 1977 – Winter 1977
	Nightingale	Summer 1980 – present
10.	Nicolette	Spring 1976 – Summer 1977
	Brunhilde	Spring 1980 – present
11.	Thistlebury	Spring 1975 – Summer 1975
	Barengaria	Fall 1975 – Spring 1979
	Bianca	Summer 1980 – present
12.	Lady Macchiavelli	Spring 1975 – Summer 1975
	Mistress Oakapple	Spring 1976 – Winter 1980
15.	Kenilworth	Fall 1975 – Summer 1976
21.	Toadflax	Summer 1977
	Chuzzlewit	Spring 1978 – Summer 1978
	Cobweb	Summer 1980
22.	Mistress Sedgwick	Fall 1976 – March 1977
	Halftail	May 1977 – July 1977
	Mistress Squatter	Fall 1977 – Winter 1978
	Salizar	Summer 1980 – present
23.	Mistress Earwicker	Fall 1976 – May 1979
24.	Willoughby	Fall 1976 – Winter 1977
	Clorindas	Summer 1979
	Tamora	Summer 1980 – present
25.	Mistress Appleford	Fall 1976 – Summer 1978
	Ariel	Fall 1979 – present
26.	Pumpkinseed	Fall 1976
	Bohort	Fall 1978 – Winter 1979
27.	Jellicle	Fall 1976 – May 1979
	Juliana	Spring 1980 – present
28.	Gustavus Adolphus	Winter 1976 – Spring 1977
	Wallenstein	Summer 1980 – present
29.	Quailfeather	Fall 1975 – Winter 1979
31/32.	Vladimir	Spring 1977 – Summer 1977
	Pilfer	Summer 1977 – Fall 1977
	Titania	Spring 1980 – present
33.	Mushroom	Spring 1977 – Summer 1977
	Peachblossom	Summer 1978 – Fall 1978
	Fiordiligi	Summer 1980 – present
34.	Ipswich	Spring 1978 – present
35.	Pellicle	Summer 1979 – present
36.	Cromwell	Summer 1979
37.	Winthrop	Spring 1979 – present
38.	Guglielmo	Summer 1980 – present

finally entered his burrow for the winter on November 28. He was not seen again until January 23, leaving Lady Cheltenham the bounty of the oak trees and the exhilaration of the winter sunshine in which she basked as the daytime temperature descended to a low of minus 2°F. She remained active in spite of cold winter rains, subfreezing and subzero temperatures, and light snow, only to retire reluctantly to her burrow between January 17 and 28, when enough snow had accumulated to make travel uncomfortable and foraging difficult.

Thus I was presented at once with the dilemma of hibernation, a dilemma that remains in spite of extensive investigation and speculation by many scientists. Why was Guilford inactive for almost two months, while Lady Cheltenham enjoyed the winter season? Hibernation, from a Latin word meaning wintering, usually implies the achievement of a torpid state during which the heart rate, breathing rate, and body temperature are all reduced to very low levels. A summary of Panuska's definition of the actual states of being that may be involved is given in figure 13. It is important to remember that a chipmunk which has retired to the burrow for the winter may be in any of these states. All we know for certain is that it is in the burrow where it cannot be observed. Consequently, opinions have varied widely as to whether or not the chipmunk is a true hibernator, capable of long periods of torpidity like the woodchuck.

It was not until laboratory studies on captive chipmunks were reported by Panuska in 1959, Richard L. Neumann in 1967, and Edward B. Pivorun in 1976 that the chipmunk's short-term hibernating talents were established. In the last study, biotelemetry was employed as temperature-sensitive radio transmitters were surgically implanted in chipmunks so that their body temperatures could be recorded in the burrow. I note this to show the sophistication of the methods that have been directed to resolving the problem. The results of these studies can be summarized by saying

that the chipmunk enters hibernation by enjoying several cycles of semitorpidity during which body temperature and breathing rate decrease in steps alternating with periods of normal activity. As the body temperature decreases, these periods of semitorpidity gradually approach the conditions of torpidity, and once this is achieved, the animal alternates between gradually lengthening periods of torpidity and normal, if sleepy, activity until three to four days of torpidity are regularly interrupted by a day of activity.

During the active periods, the chipmunk carries out its normal body functions such as eating and elimination, although it generally remains in a rather sleepy state without leaving the burrow. This restless hibernation period can last from a few days up to six or seven months. It is apparent, then, that the Eastern chipmunk is a short-term hibernator. Support for this is seen in the findings of Jack W. Hudson that during the winter, the chipmunk's thyroid gland does not show the reduced activity believed to be associated with truly hibernating animals.

Understanding the process, however, does not explain why some do it and others don't do it. During all of the winters between 1974 and 1979, a small number of chipmunks, both male and female, have remained active.

There is universal agreement in the literature that hibernation among chipmunks is unpredictable, both under controlled laboratory conditions and in the wild. For example, William L. Engels observed a male chipmunk active all winter who, after the mating season, retired between March 22 and May 2. During the final eighteen days of his inactivity, the high temperature had been 84°F. A female under similar conditions remained inactive between November 15 and May 12. Elsa Allen kept chipmunks in a large open-air pen over a five-year period during which not a single one hibernated, even though the temperature in central New York dropped to minus 20°F. One of her female

Figure 12. Gustavus Adolphus was the only chipmunk active over the winter of 1976–77.

Figure 13. States of chipmunk physiological activity (after Panuska, 1959).

State	Breathing Rate	Body Temperature	Activity
Active	> 60 per minute	35 - 41°C	
Semitorpid	20 - 60 per minute	8 - 20°C	Awake daily
Torpid	< 20 per minute	5 - 7°C	Awake every 3–4 days

Figure 14. Selected dates of winter activity for nine chipmunks over a five-year period.

	1974-75		1975-76		1976-77		1977-78		1978-79	
	In	Out	In	Out	In	Out	In	Out	In	Out
Lady Cheltenham	1-17	1-28	11-22	2-18	12-5	2-15	11-11	3-12	12-15	2-28
Gutrune			1-2	1-23	12-25	2-17				
Guinevere				2-23	11-13	2-15	11-9	2-27	11-23	3-1
Mistress Earwicker							11-8	3-22	12-26	2-3
Jellicle					12-29	2-16	11-9	3-11	12-3	2-28
Squatter							11-1	3-18	11-19	2-28
Guilford	11-28	1-23								
Fenwick			11-15	1-23	11-25	1-31	10-24	2-25	9-6?	3-3
Willoughby					12-20	1-29	10-22	3-11		

chipmunks in an outdoor cage alternated between torpidity at 55°F and activity at minus 8°F repeatedly. Some achieved at least semitorpidity in a cage in her warm kitchen. Furthermore, she observed, as I have, no constancy in the behavior of individuals from year to year. In these studies, as well as in the present one, there is no correlation between weather and hibernation.

There is even disagreement as to the existence and extent of a chipmunk's weight gain before winter inactivity. Theories such as the proposal of Grace W. Scott and Kenneth C. Fisher of "an endogenous annual rhythm, probably temperature-dependent" do not really satisfy the evidence. Fred J. Brenner and P. Dennis Lyle may have brought some light on the subject by suggesting that evolution has directed the modern chipmunk away from the hibernation pattern of its ancestors, a pattern still retained by the woodchuck, toward food hoarding as a method of winter survival. Since Allen reported higher survival rates in winteractive chipmunks as compared with those in hibernation, perhaps this is a step in the right direction.

Woodchucks have evolved to true hibernation, during which they limit winter activity and exposure to their lowest levels. Tree squirrels have evolved a combination of socialization and food storing. Chipmunks have maintained their independence by evolving to or remaining in an intermediate position in which they hoard more than enough food to offset the need for winter foraging and are able to reduce their activity significantly through partial hibernation if necessary.

But what determines the onset of hibernation? And, for that matter, what determines when awakening occurs? In my opinion, laboratory studies on captive chipmunks are biased against answering these questions, for conditions in the laboratory are far more unnatural than they may at first seem. In addition to exposing the animals to unnatural food supplies and continued contact with humans and equipment, it is well known that chipmunks do not breed in captivity and, therefore, their entire life cycle is disturbed. Furthermore, they are not allowed to hoard food to their instinctive capacity. I think that we may conclude that answers to these questions are at least temporarily beyond our understanding.

Figure 14 shows the winter activity dates

for nine chipmunks in the present study over a five-year period. For five of the nine, the period covers their entire lives. The variability is evident. During the winter of 1979–80, no one remained active. By the end of November they were all in their burrows, not to be seen again until a few emerged between March 26 and April 14 and the majority after May 17. The usual time of emergence is between late January and late February, after which the mating season begins at once.

In 1980 there was no spring mating, as the females did not come into heat and most of the males were observed to be not in breeding condition upon emergence. It is tempting to speculate that there was no mating season because they woke up too late. However, since one of the proposed theories of awakening suggests that it is in response to the arousal of the mating urge, it is even more tempting to speculate that they woke up late because there was not going to be a mating season. Thus it is, and always will be with animal studies: a speculative answer to one question only generates another frequently more complex question. The question of why there was not to be a spring mating season in 1980 is one that must be tackled in the next chapter.

3
Lady Cheltenham and Fenwick: The Mating Season

While Lady Cheltenham was enjoying her short winter rest in 1975, between January 17 and 28, Guilford was awakening from his two-month siesta. He appeared on January 23 up through the snow from a new burrow entrance about fifteen feet west of the one to which he had retired on November 28. For the next several days he appeared briefly in the early morning and early afternoon to survey the weather, and only ventured forth from his burrow when the snow was almost melted. When he finally began to move about, I could see that he was really Guilford, for he had now assumed the appearance of a mature male in breeding condition.

The male chipmunk's sexual activity is regulated to some degree physiologically, although not as precisely as is the female's. His large testicles are descended into the scrotal sac when he emerges from hibernation and his breeding appearance is quite obvious. The scrotal sac is lightly covered with fur of a shade anywhere between white and dark gray depending upon the degree of sexual maturity, the darker the color the greater the maturity. In some seasons and among some chipmunks, the testicles ascend partially into the abdomen during April, after the spring mating season. One result of this change is probably to modify the male's attitude toward females and toward the spring-born young during their helpless developmental period.

During June, the testicles descend again for the July mating season, and by late September or early October, they are completely ascended, making it difficult to distinguish the sexes in the fall. The June descent occurs even if no females come into heat, showing that the male and female sexual cycles are independent of one another.

The precise time at which male sexual maturity occurs in the spring is quite variable. On December 18, 1976, three males—Gustavus Adolphus, Willoughby, and Launcelot—were all observed to be in breeding condition two months before the mating season. At the time, Gustavus and Willoughby were both about nine months old, and Launcelot was at least twenty-one months of age. Since Willoughby became inactive between December 20 and January 29, and Launcelot retired between January 1 and February 1, both after their testicles had descended, the popular theory that hibernation ends in response to the arousal of the sexual urge would not seem to be infallible in the case of the male. On December 18 all three had been noted to have had a special interest in the few ladies that were still active.

As soon as Guilford began to travel away from his burrow, his interests became obvious. Having, presumably, a good supply of last fall's food still remaining at home, he did not forage, but spent most of his time exploring the territories of the local females, sometimes entering their burrows briefly—and frequently emerging backward quickly. In fact, several times it looked as though he had stepped on hot coals. This became his regular routine at least twice a day.

When Lady Cheltenham arose from her short rest on January 28, it was also through a new burrow entrance about six feet south of the one she had last used. She seemed less concerned than Guilford was with the snow, but she confined her activity to later in the day when the sun was high. Most of her time was spent foraging. At no time during the year is a chipmunk's antisocial nature more obvious than during this short time of activity that precedes mating in the spring.

On February 1, Guilford interrupted Lady Cheltenham's foraging with a proposition. He approached her nose-to-nose, uttering soft trills and flicking his tail up and down nervously. This tail movement, which resembles that of an angry gray squirrel, is a certain indication of a sexual proposition, for a male chipmunk engages in it only under such conditions, and I have never seen a female move her tail in this manner. Lady Cheltenham's response was swift and decisive: she pounced on Guilford with a fury unprecedented! They rolled over and over in close combat. He retreated and she pursued him relentlessly through his own territory and at least ninety feet beyond, pouncing on him again and again with unabating rage. I began to fear for his life and I suspect that he did too. When he finally escaped, she returned to her area, a picture of indignation. He was not seen again that day. I think she finally convinced him that it was neither the time nor the place.

Two inches of snow fell on February 2, followed by another six inches on February 5, and for two days only heads were seen peering briefly out of burrow entrances. By the eighth, the snow had almost melted and activity resumed with a change of heart. Lady Cheltenham and Guilford pursued each other gently through the woodpile on the back porch for almost an hour and a half. She was still not ready, however, and in the following days she seemed to become more and more preoccupied and nervous. Guilford was out each morning almost before daylight exploring Lady Cheltenham's territory and the territories of other females, but soon found himself in competition with other males who began to appear in the area to stake their claims.

Male territorial tournaments, which will be described in chapter 6, occurred frequently as the wandering males attempted to establish control over female territories in anticipation of their residents coming into heat (estrus) shortly. Being closer to home himself, Guilford managed to keep Lady Cheltenham's area under his control at first. One of the newcomers, Fenwick, a relative youngster probably born the previous spring, challenged Guilford more efficiently than the others as he excavated and moved into a simple burrow no more than twelve feet from Guilford's. Now he too could call the area home. Guilford's size, age, and experience allowed him to keep the upper hand, but Fenwick was ready when the time came.

At first light on the fifteenth, the woods erupted with activity. Everywhere, it seemed, chipmunks were chasing in tandem groups of four, five, or six. They looked like tiny freight trains chugging through the woods. Every so often the chases would break up as the female managed to elude her pursuers and the males climbed to elevated positions on tree branches or stumps in order to search for her so that the chase could be resumed. Lady Cheltenham emerged from her burrow at 7:45 and what happened during the next few minutes caused me to formulate in my mind, out of gratitude for their cooperation, this entire study and book.

She emerged during one of the break periods in a nearby chase when the males were up in the air, and Fenwick, who happened to be on top of the well, saw her at once. As she headed for the back porch almost immediately, Fenwick moved in the same direction. They met on top of the woodpile and, with no preliminary courtship, he mounted her less than six feet from the camera. In two minutes they separated, groomed their genital areas, and settled down for a four-and-a-half-hour honeymoon in the woodpile. They chased each other playfully among the logs, sat together eating, meditating, or grooming themselves for almost two hours. Occasionally, Fenwick was obliged to clear the porch of intruders as individual males who had lost a chase wandered in or as chases themselves crossed the porch. He did so very efficiently.

At 9:30 Lady Cheltenham filled her pouches with sunflower seeds and ran off to a hole that had been formed by decomposing roots in the middle of the lawn, a hole that many chipmunks used for refuge, but that no one chipmunk owned. Fenwick, followed, and they continued to chase playfully into and out of the hole, then sat together until 12:10. His defense of the area from intruders during that period was heroic. Then suddenly the honeymoon was over. Lady Cheltenham chased him away and returned to the porch. He followed her and she chased him again, more convincingly. He wandered off in search, presumably, of new conquests while she groomed and ate until 2:00 p.m., when she returned to her burrow and retired. She also scratched a lot; I think Fenwick had fleas.

This first example to which I was exposed was not a typical mating, if any mating can be said to be typical. In the next few pages I will attempt to summarize the variations in mating behavior based upon the observation of twenty-five courtships and six copulations during nine mating periods over six years. This example involved a honeymoon but no courtship. More nearly typical probably is a short courtship and a very short honeymoon.

An example of the other extreme, with a more elaborate courtship, occurred during the spring of 1979. At 10:45 on March 3 I badly needed a break from writing down descriptions of the frantic activity in the woods since daylight. I picked up the ten-power field glasses and decided to see if there was any action in the south part of the study area. As I focused through the bedroom window on a stump about sixty feet away, I saw Oakapple stretched out in what looked like a thoroughly relaxed position, looking into the woods where another chipmunk was singing. Slightly behind her and to one side, Ulysses was stretched out in the same relaxed fashion with his chin resting on her back. So they remained, perfectly still, until 11:10 when they both disappeared into the stump. An hour later, Oakapple was alone, grooming herself fastidiously.

Whether or not individual courtships can take place depends upon how many males have gotten the word that a particular female is in heat. If more than one is in the area when she decides that the time is right, a chase of sometimes monumental dimensions occurs, leaving little time for courtship when she finally selects her partner. When privacy is available, the male usually approaches the female head-on while singing soft trills and moving his tail up and down nervously. They may touch noses gently. He may nuzzle or lick her about the head and neck, under the chin, on the flank, or about the tail. She may then allow him to chase her about a small area or she may chase him pro-vocatively in a game of hide-and-seek around a hollow stump, log or brush pile, or even a tree. Each may spend periods of time perched in obscure places awaiting dis-covery. During these playful encounters, soft trills, chucking sounds, or soft chatter may be heard between them. Three exam-ples might be described to advantage, each involving different pairs.

On March 6, 1977, at 7:30 in the morning, Ulysses sat on a hollow stump and sang a chipping song for about fifteen minutes. Oakapple appeared from inside the stump and seemed to ignore him..He licked her about the head and scratched her back (no kidding) with his front paws as she continued to pay no attention. At 8:00 both entered the stump, reappearing ten minutes later to sit together for about an hour and a half before he mounted her, thrust rapidly for about two minutes, with a short rest period every few seconds, while holding her hips with his front paws. She remained prone and appeared completely passive. As they started to fall off the stump, she held on to the edge with her front paws while he hung on to her. A few seconds later they separated and were shortly interrupted by the arrival of another male, whereupon she chased them both away.

On July 25, 1978, at 7:35 a.m., Ipswich chased off Fenwick and another male and mated with Mistress Appleford on the trunk of a tree. After he had mounted her, he interrupted his thrusting every five seconds or so and was still for about five seconds. She looked about apprehensively and moved slowly up the tree as he hung on to her hips. After about a minute and a half they rolled over on their sides, a squirrel appeared, and they separated. They resumed shortly for another two minutes during which Ipswich stamped his hind feet alternately and nibbled gently at her neck while Mistress Appleford looked less apprehensive. Fenwick approached from behind but, in a rare act of courtesy, left without interfering.

After Mistress Appleford and Ipswich separated, she groomed her genital area and disappeared into the hollow base of the tree. He remained outside for some time and entered occasionally before abandoning her. At the same time, Willoughby was courting Peachblossom, a 3½-month-old juvenile, on a nearby stump. She boxed with him gently, touched his head, nuzzled him under the chin, and they touched noses. They disappeared into the stump shortly and remained for some time.

On July 31, 1978, Willoughby and Guinevere sat at 7:35 a.m. on the stump described above. Willoughby sang a chucking song very softly. Interrupted by Ipswich, they returned a few minutes later to play hide-and-seek in and around the stump, accompanied by an occasional exchange of soft chatter. Willoughby groomed his genital area frequently and always greeted Guinevere with his chucking song when she reappeared from some part of the stump.

When Fenwick approached, Willoughby chased him away with a sharp trill. He and Guinevere then chased playfully through the woods for a few minutes, ending up on top of a small concrete structure where he mounted her and engaged in intermittent thrusting for about three minutes while violently licking her neck. She seemed completely passive but became apprehensive when a dog barked. After separating, they both groomed their genitals and remained together for several minutes. During the mating, no sound was picked up by a microphone six feet above the pair. Guinevere finally returned to her burrow and Willoughby joined another chase. In this instance both locations were covered by sensitive microphones.

The details described in these examples are in general agreement with, if more complete than, the few other descriptions of mating behavior in the literature. The only notable exceptions are the occurrence of male genital grooming—which Elliott indicates as only following copulation, while it has been observed among these males generally and spontaneously throughout the periods of mating activity and for several days before any females come into heat—and multiple copulation, which has not been observed in this population. Christopher Dunford described the characteristic vertical tail flicking of courting males in his 1972 study.

When more than one male is in the female's area at the proper time, the situation is entirely different. Courtship is usually limited or nonexistent, but the honeymoon may persist. The chase that occurs under these circumstances may be initiated in a gentle or a more violent manner. For example, on February 23, 1976, Lady Cheltenham emerged from her burrow at 6:30 a.m. without observing Diarmuid, who was waiting behind her. He approached, nuzzled the back of her neck and moved off toward the woods slowly. As she followed him, Launcelot appeared and a chase erupted that was soon joined by Kenilworth and Fenwick. On February 25, 1977, Mistress Earwicker emerged at 6:25 a.m. and was quietly joined by Willoughby. As they moved off toward his area, Fenwick, Launcelot, and Rinaldo appeared and the chase was on.

By contrast, on July 25, 1975, Gutrune literally erupted from her burrow at 5:55 a.m. into the arms of Fenwick, who had been waiting patiently—but not for that. They rolled together in what looked like mortal combat into the woods where Kenilworth and Diarmiud waited to take up pursuit. At 11:30 Hannibal joined the others and was the ultimate victor, becoming the sire of Guinevere and two other youngsters.

Chases originating in this manner may last between two and nine hours. In the last example it proceeded from 6:00 a.m. until 3:00 p.m. The female's strategy seems to be to lead the males on a merry chase and eventually to surrender to the one who is able to keep up with her. Presumably he is the cleverest and the strongest. Such a procedure has obvious advantages in assessing the potential fitness of her mate. Her tactics are at once ingenious and amusing, and take somewhat different forms during the spring, when the woods are bare, and during the summer, when it is easier to hide. While observing a chase, one has to sympathize with the males as the female outmaneuvers them time after time. A favorite tactic of the female is to stop abruptly and after the males have trundled past, reverse direction while they split up and begin to search for the trail. Another is to dive headlong into a hollow log or stump and either escape through a secret opening or wait for her pursuers to funnel into an area in which they cannot all possibly fit.

During one chase, Guinevere led Fenwick, Rinaldo, and two strangers into a follow stump from which, an instant later, six chipmunks exploded in all directions. The sixth was not identified, but I bet it was surprised. The frantic nature of these chases affects the whole neighborhood. In one instance a gray squirrel was seen wandering innocently into the middle of a chase. It fled to the top of a tree in what appeared to be abject terror.

During the chase, vocalization is common. Growls, squeals, and chattering are heard frequently along with a high-pitched whistle that resembles a shriek but may continue for five seconds or more and is only heard during mating chases. The chipmunks move too swiftly for the speaker to be identified, but whether the sound is produced by the male or the female, it serves to attract the other males in the neighborhood, thereby providing the female with a wider choice.

Since the female is so clever at evading her pursuers, they spend most of their time trying to find her. They frequently climb to elevated positions in order to do so and just as frequently return to her territory to begin the search anew. One of them can generally be seen guarding her entrance throughout the chase, and the guard may be changed regularly. They will also enter her burrow, often to find it vacant. This is what probably stimulated John Burroughs's famous comment: "What a train of suitors she had that day!" She was probably not at home.

During the summer season the tactics are more finely honed, as there is more cover in which the female can hide. At this time, chases are more likely to include both large and small trees. One of the favorite places in the Cheltenham Chipmunk Refuge to which females almost invariably lead their processions is an area of dense brush, about thirty feet in diameter, that must be almost completely darkened by a thick canopy of honeysuckle. A microphone over this areas has revealed many secrets.

Two examples of summer tactics are worth mentioning; both occurred on July 25, 1980. Brunhilde, having temporarily eluded her pursuers, appeared in the open beneath a tree. Approached from behind, she leapt into the air, landing a few feet away in the brush, and disappeared. She reappeared at the same spot within a few seconds and, so effectively had her suitor been confused, a full thirty seconds passed before he returned.

Later that afternoon, Dierdre was seen crossing forty-five feet of open lawn, her body hugging the ground while four males searched frantically within eighteen inches of her. Clorindas finally located her and approached, singing a series of trills and flicking his tail vertically, while Ipswich watched from three feet away. Dierdre moved away several times before permitting Clorindas to mount and begin thrusting. Ipswich continued to watch for five seconds before attempting to interrupt. Clorindas snapped at him without releasing her, but on Ipswich's second attack, he dismounted and chased his ungentlemanly companion thirty feet up a tree while Dierdre moved about six feet away in the grass. When Clorindas returned fifteen seconds later, he was unable to locate her after searching over a very wide area. He seemed annoyed by the incident, but not wildly upset.

During these frantic chases, females that are not in heat generally go about their business and are not molested. They frequently remain close to home, defending their territories with little effect as the chases cross them. Since the chase positions teeth close to tails, the inevitable result is sometimes seen. Ipswich returned from his adventures on July 27, 1980, with half of his tail gone. Although I am sure it was a blow to his ego, such anatomical modifications are of great help to an observer in identifying individuals.

It seems appropriate at this point to mention how it is possible to identify individuals, especially at a distance and in rapid motion. I do not claim, as D. K. Scott did with swans, to be able to recognize 450 chipmunks on sight. She was able to achieve up to 97 percent accuracy even from color slides. However, intimate observation with chipmunks that, to the casual observer, may all look alike proves that familiarity breeds recognition rather than contempt. No two chipmunks are exactly alike. They differ in size, body shape, coloring, coat design (pelage), as well as in behavior. The way they move, their characteristic postures are all different. Their self-confidence and attitude toward other chipmunks, and even toward humans, sometimes serve to distinguish them. There are two features that are most useful in this respect: facial expression, which results from a combination of head shape and the markings about the eyes and cheeks rather than from disposition, and tail shape, the most useful distinguishing feature from a distance, especially after modification.

A chipmunk may have a long tail or a short tail, a broad tail or a thin tail, a dark tail or a light tail, a straight tail or a crooked tail, a blunt tail or a pointed tail, a blade-shaped tail that is broad at its base and tapers toward its tip or a spatulate tail that is broad at its tip and tapers toward its base, a tail that curves upward or a tail that curves downward, a tail finely furred or a tail coarsely furred, and on and on. A damaged tail may assume an absolutely unique appearance. A characteristic but slight fraying at the tip from a benign encounter must be viewed with caution, as it may change when the chipmunk molts or changes its coat, but severe damage always results in the outgrowth of a tuft of fur at the healed tip that becomes the possession of only one chipmunk.

Fenwick, who may have wanted a lock of her hair for a souvenir, removed about a third of an inch of Lady Cheltenham's tail during her second season. The characteristic tuft that grew out had a forked appearance that remained through the last four seasons of her life. She got even with him about a month later when she bit the center of his tail. She apparently damaged the bone structure but did not break it, for if she had the end would eventually have fallen off. Nevertheless, he lost partial control of the end half of the tail, and thereafter it always had a flaglike appearance that was obvious from 150 feet away. It actually added to his rakish image.

Quailfeather lost half of her tail to Lady Cheltenham's sharp teeth during an argument over some sunflower seeds. The flesh and fur were stripped from the bone and the exposed vertebrae fell off about a day later. Within a month she had grown a black tuft of fur that became her mark.

These are only a few examples of obvious differences in appearance, and the reader may be reassured that close and continuous observation will reveal the small scars and subtle differences in stripe pattern that characterize each chipmunk as an individual.

The mating behavior that has been described occurs only during brief periods in the chipmunk's annual season, indicating what is called synchronous estrus or simply that all females come into heat at about the same time. The reproductive physiology of the Eastern chipmunk has been treated in detail in a study by Lorraine and Donald Smith. The appearance of the vaginal opening of a female chipmunk in heat is quite obvious—that is, if you can get her to raise her tail, which she is usually not disposed to do at this time. It becomes enlarged and inflamed, returning to normal a few days later. The estrus period for a particular female seems to be confined to one day. On this day, although she may be physiologically compelled to mate, she still maintains otherwise complete control over the situation, as she is

Figures 17–20 (clockwise from top left). A study in tails: Ipswich after the chase, sans tail; Fenwick's flaglike tail; Lady Cheltenham's trademark; Quailfeather's tufted appendage

able to outsmart the males so easily and is free to choose the partner and place. Although she may seem thoroughly persecuted, I have never seen a female injured during mating. Males, on the other hand, frequently leave the mating season lame, scarred, or tailless.

The mating seasons in this area of Virginia usually occur during the last two weeks in February and July although, in some years, the spring season has occurred as much as a month later. The dates of the summer season are more reliable, but the season itself is not. Figure 21 shows the mating records of four females under direct and intimate observation; they represent the other females as well. The dates are those on which the young chipmunks emerged from the burrow. These litters resulted from matings that had occurred

about ten weeks earlier. In the summer of 1975 fewer than half of the resident females mated, and during the summers of 1977 and 1979 none of them did. In only one of the six years studied, 1980, was there no spring mating.

During 1980, emergence from hibernation was not complete until the second week in May, and there was neither mating activity observed nor did any juveniles appear during the summer. In fact, many of the males were not in breeding condition when they emerged, giving rise to outrageous identification problems. The summer mating season proceeded on schedule, however, with apparently all of the eligible females coming into heat. There was, then, no reproductive activity for fifteen months between March 1979 and July 1980.

Figure 21. *Mating record of four female chipmunks.*

	Lady Cheltenham	Gutrune	Guinevere b. 3-75	Mistress Earwicker b. 8-76
1975 Spring	5-3 (4) Fenwick*	5-4 (3)		
Summer	—	10-4 (3) Hannibal		
1976 Spring	5-4 (6) Fenwick	5-2 (5) Launcelot	4-28 (4)	
Summer	9-28 (5) Launcelot	9-28 (6) Transient 26	9-27 (3) Kenilworth	
1977 Spring	5-13 (6)	5-3 (4) Fenwick	5-1 (4) Fenwick	5-12 (4) Willoughby
Summer	—	— (d. 8-77)	—	—
1978 Spring	5-30 (6)		5-11 (4) Chuzzlewit	5-28 (4) Ipswich
Summer	11-24 (?) Ipswich		10-16 (?) Willoughby	10-5 (?) Willoughby
1979 Spring	Mated with Bohort 3-4 (d. 3-79)		5-16 (?) Bohort —	5-16 (6) Ipswich (d. 7-79)

*Date of litter emergence (number in litter) Sire.

The question why is a difficult but interesting one, and it might be tempting to invoke the eruption of Mount St. Helens or the chipmunk's overindulgence in a diet of cicada during the summer of 1979 as explanations. As will be discussed in chapter 7, it has been theorized—and sometimes demonstrated in other mammals—that the increased frequency of encounters as the population grows, produces stress that may inhibit reproductive activity and, thus, control the population. As will also be seen later, this could explain why there was no summer mating season in 1977, when the population was the most dense of the six studied years. In the fall of 1979, however, the population had been decreasing for two years, so I am afraid the question does not have an obvious answer, but rather one that may require a study of longer than six years.

That there are exceptions to the precise dates of the mating seasons was suggested by Elsa Allen, who described a female that was in lactation again a few months after she had lost her spring litter. In July 1975 I observed a six-week-old juvenile from what must have been a mid-April mating. On November 24, 1978, Lady Cheltenham still had at least one juvenile in her burrow. This youngster must have resulted from an unobserved mating in early September. The mother had been the object of male interest in late July and again in late August. It is probably not pertinent to this discussion, since he was not in breeding condition on November 9, 1975, but Fenwick was seen courting a 3½-month-old juvenile female.

In view of the chipmunk's well-documented solitary existence, late mating in the fall may explain the few literary observations, mostly before 1900, of several chipmunks in a winter-excavated burrow in colder climates. If the young from a late mating were not ready to leave the burrow by the time the mother was ready for hibernation, say in October, they may have had to spend the winter hibernating in the home burrow themselves. By December or January, when the reported burrows were opened, the young would have been full grown and a communal existence might have suggested itself.

In more northern climates the spring season has been reported to occur during March and April, but the summer season appears to favor July throughout the range. Two seasons have been confirmed in New York, Michigan, Ohio, Indiana, Ontario, and Ottawa. Only one season has been reported in Wisconsin and Minnesota.

A final consideration concerning reproductive behavior is the age of sexual maturity, that is, the age at which chipmunks are capable of breeding. The observation of chipmunks can only answer the question of at what age they actually do breed, since the female obviously does not breed until she comes into heat for the first time. At this time it is also possible for the male to breed, although he could be physiologically ready earlier. After reviewing much evidence, the Smiths concluded that females are mature at 2½ to 3 months of age and males at 9 to 11 months. William H. Burt and Ralph Yerger both have reported that spring-born females appear to breed during their first summer.

The mating of Peachblossom, born in early April, on July 25, 1978, when she was photographed in heat, indicates a minimum age of 3½ months, since that is the shortest time period between birth and the first available mating season. If a spring-born female does not mate at 3½ months of age, she will have to wait until she is 11 months old for the next available mating season. Four summer-born females—Appleford, Earwicker, Jellicle, and Oakapple—all mated at six months of age the following spring.

In agreement with published reports, spring-born males in this area do not appear in breeding condition before December of the same year, and mate successfully the following spring. Summer-born males may be in breeding condition the following spring, but they do not usually mate as successfully as the older, more experienced, males. Bohort, born in August 1978, was an exception.

Having swept Lady Cheltenham off her feet, Fenwick went on to achieve notable success during the rest of the spring 1975 mating season. By March 1, when the woods had quieted down, he emerged as the leading citizen, who commanded the respect of the entire population, while Lady Cheltenham turned her attention to the domestic scene with the anticipation of the birth of her family.

4

Lady Cheltenham's Family

As Lady Cheltenham retired from the political scene at the end of the mating season, Fenwick succeeded to the position of dominance in the community. His flag-like tail became the banner of his authority as he ejected one and all, including Lady Cheltenham, from the favored feeding sites. His competitive relationship with Guilford deteriorated to one of intense irritation, and the two fought as frequently as possible. The deciding factor was Fenwick's growing self-confidence.

In early March, Guilford appeared with a wound on his left cheek, which had apparently been caused by a puncture of the pouch and which apparently resulted in his demise from a septic infection. He was not seen after March 24, and Gutrune, a very large and domineering female, was observed using his burrow on March 26, just before she delivered her spring litter.

This event represented one of only two observations during the six years of a female changing quarters. Where she had come from or why she had moved are difficult to explain, but may be rationalized. Had she experienced some disaster in her former home? Perhaps she had escaped from a blacksnake that had entered the burrow and, in her advanced state of pregnancy, considered the survival of her young more important than the home and supplies she had left behind. Probably none of this took place, but the move was an instinctive response for the survival of herself and her family. The other observation occurred in 1979 when Mistress Earwicker moved a distance of about fifteen feet into the burrow of her mother, Lady Cheltenham, after the latter's death. This, however, was the burrow in which she had been raised. Gutrune had certainly not grown up in Guilford's burrow.

After the mating season, Lady Cheltenham's behavior changed dramatically much like Brunhilde's domestication in the *Nibelungenlied* after Siegfried awakens her from the magic fire. She spent most of her time elaborating her burrow, opening new entrances and carrying in large quantities of leaves for bedding material. Her diet tended toward animal matter and she began storing more provisions in the burrow. She even began stealing food from other burrows, particularly Guilford's and Fenwick's. The signs of pregnancy began to show about three weeks later when it became obvious that she was putting on weight, and signs of mammary development and lactation were obvious after four weeks.

It was shortly after she had raised this litter that Lady Cheltenham became sufficiently friendly to eat out of my hand, but during each succeeding pregnancy she became hostile and refused to have anything to do with me. This hostility lasted from the third week of gestation to the day before she let the youngsters out of the burrow nine weeks later. Thus I could always tell when youngsters would appear, and be in place to photograph them. Since they saw me when they first emerged, they had no fear of me.

As her pregnancy progressed, Lady Cheltenham became more timid away from her burrow and territory, but more ferocious in defending her territory against intruders. She frequently seemed to prepare remote burrow entrances for the use of the youngsters, but she never used them. They always emerged from her current entrance and used it exclusively until they were dispersed. The only exception to the exclusive use of the home burrow entrance was presented on two occasions by Mistress Earwicker, who spent the summer of 1978 stocking and elaborating Willoughby's abandoned burrow, although she always spent the night in her own. As soon as her young emerged from the burrow on Octo-

Figure 22. Gutrune twenty-seven days pregnant.

ber 5, she moved them into Willoughby's, from which they were later dispersed. This naturally left your zealous author and his camera firmly established in the wrong place.

In the spring of the following year when her litter emerged on May 16 from her burrow, she immediately moved them into Lady Cheltenham's nearby abandoned burrow, from which they were dispersed on June 15, and into which she herself moved shortly. The observations by Elliott of young chipmunks emerging from quarters other than the natal burrow raise the question of how the mother moves the children from home to their emergence burrow without their having emerged to get there.

The gestation period lasts thirty-one days. The mother enters confinement, to use the Victorian term, from four to seven days before birth and reappears one to twenty days later. The birth of litters resulting from captive matings has been described by Elsa Allen. The young are born one at a time about fifteen to twenty minutes apart. Each is carefully washed by the mother with her tongue before being deposited in the nest.

The litter size varies from one to nine, with four or five being average. This has been determined by dissection and counting the embryos or placental scars. The

number of juveniles that emerge seven weeks later may not account for all that were born, since some may not survive. The thorough wildness of the Eastern chipmunk is demonstrated by the fact that observation of birth and development has only been possible with captive-mated females. Wild-mated females, captured during pregnancy, invariably destroy their young shortly after birth or at best leave them unattended.

The young are born helpless, naked, and with their eyes and ears closed. Their development, as described by Allen, is shown in figure 23. Lorraine and Donald

Figure 23. Development of the young Eastern chipmunk (after Allen, 1938).

Age (days)	Approximate Weight (g)	Activity
1	5	Squeal
5	10	Lower teeth show
6		Stripes show
7		Hair shows
10	15	Move about
22		Ears open
30	30	Eyes open, fully furred, weaned
40	60	Emerge from burrow
60	>80	Growth attained
100		Females sexually mature

Figure 24. Jellicle in lactation, ten days postpartum.

Smith have also described aspects of chipmunk growth and development.

When the mother chipmunk reappears after parturition, she seldom spends more than fifteen minutes out of the burrow, but may venture forth several times during the day to forage and defend her territory or just to get away from the kids for a while. Her defensive ferocity reaches its peak during this period. In chapter 5 I describe in detail what happened one day when Lady Cheltenham returned home from one of her expeditions to find Launcelot in the burrow with her six youngsters. Needless to say he was not welcome, but males do seem to show a great deal of curiosity concerning the litters even when they are not the fathers. The periods of time spent by the mother away from the burrow gradually lengthen and after the thirtieth day, the time of weaning, she may begin remaining out all day, from dawn to dusk, although she will return to the entrance frequently to check on the kids.

During these postweaning days, females may engage in what has been referred to as scatter-hoarding, that is, hiding food carefully in several locations in or near her territory. She apparently does not want to return home and give her youngsters the opportunity to attempt to nurse. At the end of the day she can be counted upon to recover these hidden provisions and carry them home before dark.

A plump Lady Cheltenham disappeared into her burrow on March 13, 1975, the twenty-sixth day of her pregnancy, and reappeared just as plump, but obviously in lactation, on March 19, the thirty-second day, or one day after the young should have been born. She behaved essentially as described above during the ensuing weeks, and late in the afternoon of May 3, four 46-day-old youngsters appeared from her burrow, first singly, then in pairs, trios, and finally all together while she watched from nearby. The emergence of this particular litter was a bit later than the average of forty-two days after birth.

The youngsters were approximately two-thirds their mother's size. Young chipmunks can easily be distinguished from adults by a combination of several features. Even after they have attained adult size, their heads appear longer and leaner, with more prominent ears. The coats are silky, the tails perfect and perhaps a bit thinner than the adults', and the lower, dark cheek stripes are well defined. As the juveniles mature, these stripes become diffuse.

The first order of business for the youngsters upon emergence is to see as much of the world as possible without leaving the security of the burrow entrance. This results in their pushing one another about in order to gain a favored position, a procedure frequently resembling the movement of the chorus in a Greek tragedy or the flag raising on Iwo Jima. As I mentioned earlier, if a human is present when they first emerge, young chipmunks seem to consider him a part of the normal world at large and, if he keeps still, generally ignore him. Being there at the right time makes it much easier for the observer to photograph the antics of the youngsters, and they can even be watched without cover, although some modest camouflage allows the photographer to move about and manipulate the camera without distracting them from their explorations.

The mother usually cooperates by watching carefully from a distance, if she can be enticed out of the burrow before her offspring. If the youngsters try to emerge first, the mother may sense the presence of the observer and prevent them from leaving the burrow. She is quite sensitive to ground vibrations. These habits are based upon the chipmunk's reticence to enter the burrow when watched for fear of giving away its location, a reticence observed but not explained by Burroughs. Consequently, if the mother is allowed to emerge and go about her business, the observer can take his place and await the youngsters while the mother watches without interfering.

During the six years of this study, Lady Cheltenham was the only exception to the rule. She was the only female chipmunk that would remain at the burrow entrance with her youngsters while observed and the illustrations of maternal behavior all involve her litters. See colorplate 5 (page 23) for a family portrait of Lady Cheltenham with five-sixths of her May 1976 litter. Five youngsters can be seen to have their hind feet either in or on the edge of the two-inch burrow entrance; there simply was not room for the sixth above ground. It probably had someone's feet planted on its head.

During the first day or two after emergence, the youngsters generally remain within eighteen inches of the entrance, gazing at their new world with curiosity and alertness. Figure 25 shows how quickly they realize the effectiveness of elevation in extending their visual range. The mother chipmunk may act quite maternally at this time, appearing to draw the attention of her offspring to interesting sights, although often without much influence (figs. 26 and 27). She may chase one home if it wanders too far afield, and even put on a show of threatening intruders (fig. 28). The intruder in this case was the photographer's daughter.

Discipline may be stern, and it is sometimes not possible to say what terrible crime the errant child has perpetrated. Like humans, the extent of the discipline exerted is quite variable, and in this respect Lady Cheltenham was only average. Gutrune

Figure 25. Lady Cheltenham's youngsters look at the world from their full height.

would spend the first day or two in a watchful position near the entrance, preventing her children from leaving it. As soon as more than shoulders appeared above the ground she would dash to the entrance and violently stomp the youngsters back in with her forepaws. After the second day she apparently realized the futility of this over-protectiveness and left them pretty much to their own devices while she herself wandered about the business of foraging. Guinevere, Gutrune's daughter, appeared to exert no discipline at all, permitting the children to wander freely from the first day. She only snapped at them when they got in her way.

Mistress Squatter, whose burrow was located in open lawn and therefore was under threat from aerial predators, always stayed with the litter throughout the post-emergence period. Jellicle, whose burrow was located on the edge of the state road, seemed to exert very little discipline, but during her three seasons managed to keep her youngsters off the road. None was ever found to have succumbed to the traffic as she herself did, ironically, in the spring of 1979. What degree of discipline is ideal is difficult to say since all seemed quite successful in raising families.

After the second day, the youngsters begin to move away from the burrow entrance in order to explore their surroundings more widely. They also begin interacting with one another in small groups as they explore. The mother is less able to give them individual attention, but now assumes the difficult job of keeping track of them. It sometimes seems as though she can count.

One evening in May 1976 as darkness approached, Lady Cheltenham rounded up her six little savages and led them home to the burrow. She entered and five of them followed. The sixth hesitated at the entrance and then wandered off into the brush. A few seconds later mother reappeared, looked and listened for a moment, then scampered into the brush in pursuit, returning shortly, followed by the lost child. She reentered the burrow, but since the rebellious youngster hesitated again, she reappeared a second time, picked up the youngster in her teeth by the scruff of the neck and literally stuffed it into the burrow. She then followed, having convinced one and all that the day had ended. The following evening the same scenario was reenacted.

During this stage in the education of young chipmunks, communication—which will be discussed in more detail in the next chapter—may achieve its most sophisticated level. Mother and young can frequently be heard chattering at one another. One morning in May 1975 four youngsters were playing in the burrow entrance and listening to Lady Cheltenham sing her regular chipping song a few feet away. Suddenly the song's pitch dropped about a quarter of a tone and instantly the four disappeared into the burrow. Mother sang six more measures and disappeared after them. A few seconds later a rabbit hopped out of the brush and across the territory.

One afternoon in May 1976 Launcelot, a rather scruffy and belligerent male who resided about thirty feet behind Lady Cheltenham's territory, attacked one of her youngsters at the entrance to the natal burrow. After a brief scuffle, the youngster escaped into the brush and Launcelot

*Figures 26 and 27 (opposite). Lady Chelten-
ham attempts to instruct her child; the
latter prefers to be affectionate.*

*Figure 28 (right). Mother—the guardian of
a new generation—snarls at potential
danger.*

entered the burrow briefly. He emerged and
took up a waiting position in the brush
about three feet from the entrance. Lady
Cheltenham returned without observing
him and went to the youngster who had
been attacked. Meanwhile, a second
youngster had followed Launcelot out of
the burrow and sat in the entrance staring
at the invader. As soon as Lady Cheltenham returned to the entrance a moment
later, the second youngster attacked
Launcelot and was joined instantly in the
chase by its mother. The timing was too
nearly perfect to be coincidental. Young
chipmunks are not cowards, at least not
when mother is around. On another
occasion, someone appeared from the
woods behind Lady Cheltenham's territory.
She attacked with a flying leap into the
brush and three brave youngsters waddled
after her into the jaws of peril.

Since the emergence of litters is more or
less simultaneous, the wrong parents and
children occasionally encounter each other
during this period of wandering. Problems
seldom arise. One day, one of Mistress
Earwicker's children approached one of
Lady Cheltenham's at its burrow about
fifteen feet away. Lady Cheltenham's
youngster watched without blinking as its
niece or nephew fled home. On another
day, Mistress Earwicker herself approached
three of Lady Cheltenham's kids to a
distance of only one foot. Two of the
children retired into the burrow, but the
third stared its half sister down and
Mistress Earwicker went home. When one of
Gutrune's youngsters scaled a tree stump
in the woods and found its adult half sister
Guinevere in possession, it leaped backward into the air and raced home in panic.

As the youngsters travel farther away
from home, they are sometimes accompanied by their mother. In the spring of
1978 one of Mistress Earwicker's children
tended to follow its mother about as she
foraged. This was unusual, for generally the
mother discourages it by leaving her
territory quickly, so that the youngsters
do not have the opportunity to follow. One
day she ran to the porch with her young
chaperone trailing behind. Every twelve or
fifteen feet the youngster began to move
ahead of its mother and she had to grasp it
firmly around the shoulders with her forepaws in order to slow it down. Mistress
Squatter, whose burrow was on the open
lawn and who was therefore quite protective of her family, used to herd three or
four at a time from one feeding site to
another without ever seeming to lose track
of them. Eventually, the juveniles tire of
being watched so carefully and make quite
a game of hiding from their mother. She
may finally leave them to find their own
way home, which they do without difficulty.

One day in the summer of 1980, one of
Juliana's youngsters followed its mother to
the porch to forage in the two-inch-deep
layer of sunflower seed hulls that carpeted
the floor. Whenever Juliana approached,
the youngster buried its head ostrichlike in
the seed hulls and remained motionless.
The trick seemed to work, for each time
Juliana returned to her foraging at once.
During this period of wandering, the
females are frequently seen carrying leaves
into holes that have no history of use as
burrows. One might suspect that they are
preparing residences for the young or
possibly for themselves if life becomes too
hectic at home. However, I have never seen

either youngsters or adults use these residences.

The social behavior among littermates, which is most intensive during the third to sixth days after emergence, has been described by Elliott and to a lesser extent by the Henisches. Elliott's descriptions arise from remote-controlled still photography. While the narrative that follows generally agrees with the previous reports, it arises from the continuous observation and still photography of sixteen litters from distances of less than fifteen feet. As I have pointed out previously, the observer's presence at the moment of initial emergence conditions the young to his continued presence, providing he does not attempt to hide himself too carefully, but only to the extent that his manipulation of camera and tape recorder are not distracting. He wants only to avoid having the youngsters stop and stare at him every time he moves the camera or scratches a fresh mosquito bite. Incidentally, most of the photographs were taken using an electronic flash of about 1/3000-second duration. After two, or at the most three, flashes, the young chipmunks were completely habituated to both the light and the sound of the shutter and paid no further attention to either.

On May 6, 1975, after Lady Cheltenham's four youngsters had exhausted all of the group postures and rearrangements at the entrance to their natal burrow and had explored their immediate environment of ground litter, flowers, the little red flags that had been placed by the photographer to mark their present and previous burrow entrances, and all of the other edible and inedible objects, they began to show an interest in one another and commenced their exploration of the nature of chipmunks. Less carefully attended and supervised by their mother now, they turned to their siblings for the brief and exclusive period of companionship of their soon to be solitary lives.

Having but two or three days to find out what they themselves are all about, as reflected in their companions, young chip-

Figures 29–31 (opposite). Mutual explora-tion: young chipmunks engaged in discover-ing what chipmunks are all about. From top to bottom: one of Gutrune's offspring feels the head of a sibling; two of Gutrune's youngsters appear to be dancing; and two of Lady Cheltenham's children examine each other carefully.

munks make the most of physical explora-tion—tactile, nasal, and oral—about all parts of the body but mostly confined to the mouth, eyes, and head in general (see figs. 29–31, colorplate 8, and frontispiece). When we realize that they will never have another opportunity to examine chip-munks amicably at such close quarters, we can recognize the importance of this period to the development of their self-image in whatever form it takes. Even though this behavior may be described as play, it is very serious business. Having discovered what they—in the mirror of their siblings—smell, taste, and feel like, they begin to interact more aggressively. The mounting behavior so important later in sexual encounters is acted out as they climb upon one another's backs (fig. 32) in what appears to be a demonstration of affection. Both Elliott and I have wondered about the possible sexual connotations of this common behavior, but we have not been able to determine the sex of the performers. Sex determination at this age would require handling, an act that would place in doubt the validity of any further observation of the behavior of a particular litter.

During the following days, play becomes more aggressive as they sit up on their hind feet and box (fig. 33), and gradually the truculence of independence begins to appear as a dominance pattern emerges within the litter. The skirmishes become more competitive and biting begins to take the place of wrestling and boxing (figs. 34 and 35). While these skirmishes occur between two individuals, other members of the litter frequently watch carefully, not seeming to want to become involved, and possibly learning from the tactics of their brothers and sisters. Whether or not they Monday-morning-quarterback these tactics is something we will never know. When the skirmishes begin to terminate in chases followed by avoidance, and when squeals and growls appear in the scenario, we know that independence is just around the corner. During this period—the second post-emergence week—the mother becomes

Figure 32. Mounting behavior: Guinevere's offspring.

Figure 33. Guinevere's youngsters box.

Figures 34 and 35. Shortly before dispersal, Mistress Squatter's children fight playfully (left); then play turns to aggression.

decidedly less tolerant of the litter's presence, snapping at them and chasing them frequently. This is another indication of impending dispersal.

Having learned to suffer one another ungraciously, the final determinant of independence is the youngster's achievement of a kind equilibrium or self-confidence in its environment. The single most obvious event in this adaptation seems to be the youngster's acquisition of the ability to climb. Even though young chipmunks scurry up and down trees from about the third day out, their talents in this respect are less than deft (colorplate 9, page 67). Once they have mastered the negotiation of three-dimensional space, they are ready for the real world.

I have been unable to confirm objectively the very strong impressions in my mind that another dispersal signal arises from the young chipmunk's acquisition of an awareness that when danger threatens, it is more practical to hide in the immediate area than to run home to the burrow. Given the importance of the secrecy of the burrow entrance to the chipmunk's safety, and given the tendency of the newly emerged youngster to seek the security of home when frightened, this factor would logically seem important. Unless they are situated in the burrow entrance at the time, adult chipmunks always hide in the nearest hole, hollow log, or tree, rather than expose the location of their living quarters by running home from danger.

Depending upon the independence of the offspring and the tolerance of the mother, the act of dispersal may be abrupt or gradual. Anywhere between five and twenty days after emergence, but most generally about two weeks, we may simply observe no youngsters appearing from the natal burrow one morning. In fact, we may never see them again if they have all left the area. Mother put her foot (paw?) down and simply did not allow them into the burrow the previous evening.

Frequently, however, dispersal may take several days, depending on how clever the mother is in keeping them out and how clever the youngsters are in sneaking in. Although she gladly chases them from her territory, I have never seen a mother chipmunk chase a youngster out of the burrow itself. Consequently, one or more members of the litter may succeed in sneaking into the house during the evening—perhaps while the mother is chasing another from the territory—and thereby earn another night's lodging. The fewer that remain, however, the harder this is to accomplish, and eventually the mother is alone. The timing of all of these family events— mating, birth, emergence, dispersal—is shown for four females throughout most or all of their lives in Appendix E. Edwin R. Pidduck and J. Bruce Falls have presented some similar information in their study of chipmunk reproduction and emergence in Canada.

Newly dispersed chipmunks must move swiftly in order to find a temporary or permanent home, for they become the prey of both predators and adult chipmunks. Even though they can count upon not being eaten by their adult kind, they are chased ferociously from existing territories and spend much of their time hiding in the grass. Drainpipes are another favorite hiding place. Since the local domestic cats seem to know when the young chipmunks are afoot and homeless, I have endured nights with every roof drain on the house occupied by chipping young chipmunks, each watched carefully by a neighbor's cat. I can usually count on having to go out and chase the cats in order to get a night's sleep.

Many juveniles move into unoccupied burrows at once, while others are seen still hiding food locally several months later, an indication that whatever home they have is only temporary. The construction of a new burrow, although less common than the occupation of an abandoned existing one, is a time-consuming operation.

How far dispersed chipmunks may travel before finding a home is a question that has, to some degree, been answered by E. F. Roberts and D. P. Snyder. In a cleverly designed experiment they injected lactating females with radioactive iodine. As a result, the iodine was incorporated into the proteins of the mother's milk and hence into the body proteins of the youngsters who consumed the milk, allowing the young of a particular female to be identified upon capture by their radioactivity for several months after emergence and dispersal. These studies revealed that one or two from a litter may settle very close to the mother's territory, while all of the others disappear completely from the thirty-acre study area. Observations in the present study have been similar up to the point to which they can be interpreted.

In the fall of 1975, of Gutrune's three youngsters, only Guinevere remained in a burrow about thirty feet from her natal burrow. In the fall of 1976, of Lady Cheltenham's five youngsters, Mistress Earwicker established herself in a new burrow about fifteen feet from home and Willoughby occupied an abandoned burrow forty-five feet away. In the spring of 1977, Pilfer, from a litter of four, settled about sixty feet from Gutrune's house. He was named for what he did to his mother's food supply that summer. In the spring of 1979, Clorindas moved into Willoughby's abandoned burrow, while his mother, Mistress Earwicker, dispersed the other five and moved into Lady Cheltenham's burrow. Later that summer he moved into the ancestral home after his mother's death.

During the same year, Juliana remained in her mother's burrow after Jellicle was run over on the road. Pellicle, also from Jellicle's litter of five, occupied a new burrow on the edge of the road about forty-five feet away. Pickwick, Oakapple, Mistress Squatter, and Jellicle herself all settled in the area from separate local litters, whose numbers were not determined. In every case, the other littermates seemed to disappear completely from the area.

The dispersal of the young is aided by a particular and fascinating phenomenon. Both casual and serious naturalists have observed for many years that chipmunks sing in chorus for about a week during the late spring and again in the early fall. The chip-chip-chip of sometimes dozens of chipmunks fills the woods throughout the day. Although the animals may or may not know why they do this, it all seems to serve useful purposes.

Behaviorists use the term "epideictic display" to describe a message given by individuals to other members of a population that reveals their own existence and permits others to know the density of the population. The term is somewhat redundant since the word *epideictic* itself means shown off or displayed, particularly with reference to oratory. Furthermore, to behaviorists it carries the connotation of altruism, behavior that benefits others at the expense of the animal exhibiting it. The altruistic connotation arises from the belief by some that the display leads to voluntary curtailment of reproduction or voluntary dispersal, both for the purpose of regulating population density, a belief advanced by V. C. Wynne-Edwards and dismissed by Edward O. Wilson.

The Greek word from which *epideictic* is derived usually means simply to show off. Plato used it very cleverly in his Socratic dialogue *Protagoras*. The title character of this dialogue is supposed to be the most articulate of the Sophists, a school of philosophers for which neither Plato nor Socrates had much use. Plato used the word in many forms to indicate that, whether Protagoras was illustrating his point with a story or by logical development, he was doing little more than showing off oratorical and rhetorical skills. In some of their other writings, both Plato and Herodotus used the original word in an even more selfish context to mean to show off or display for oneself or what is one's own, in other words, in a territorial context. This is so close to the nonaltruistic interpretation of the chipmunk's dispersal chorus that I prefer to use the term *epideictic vocalization*, rather than display, to describe it.

The adult chipmunks, the orators, appear to be declaiming their territorial rights selfishly, while the dispersing juveniles, the listeners, almost certainly need to know, again selfishly, when they have reached an area with enough elbow room for a happy and fruitful existence. There is no altruism involved. Although the juveniles may not be able to count the voices, they can certainly judge the volume level and complexity of the chorus to the necessary extent. It may serve additionally to their safety during migration.

Predators, which seem to be quite aware of the dispersal and the opportunities it affords for a meal of tender young chipmunk, need to be able to concentrate on stalking their prey. Like the Light Brigade, they have chipmunks to the left of them and chipmunks to the right of them singing their hearts out, but seem to be unable to charge into the valley of gourmet dining, for it requires too many choices. On these mornings I have, at dawn, seen domestic cats with greed in their eyes slink into the woods only to leave empty-mouthed an hour later looking thoroughly exasperated.

Since dispersal restores all chipmunks to their normal state of independence and to their typical solitary behavior, what can be said about the postdispersal relationship between the mother and her juveniles who remain in the area? Mistress Earwicker, who settled indiscreetly close to her mother's house, was always a source of irritation to Lady Cheltenham, and their feuding gave no indication that they were family.

Guinevere, on the other hand, was the only observed exception. Between her territory and her mother's there was a tree stump that many chipmunks used as the last stopping place before dashing to the well with its adjacent dogwood tree and thence to the porch. Gutrune would sit by her entrance about fifteen feet from this stump and instantly launch a savage chase and attack at any chipmunk arriving on it. She knew that the well was their next destination, and would sometimes move so as to intercept the invader there. However, when it was Guinevere who appeared on the stump, Gutrune always seemed to hesitate for almost a second before pursuing and, consequently, never caught her daughter. Furthermore, she always began a direct chase, never attempting

to head Guinevere off at the well. Had
I not known that they were mother and
daughter, this observed behavior would
have been overlooked. It would have been
logical to assume simply that Guinevere
was faster on her feet than Gutrune. So
there may indeed be a slight but permanent
family bond among some chipmunks.

On the morning of May 15, 1975, Lady
Cheltenham appeared from her burrow
alone, climbed to a low tree branch nearby
and joined the chorus. On May 20 she was
alone in the silent woods.

5

Lady Cheltenham Alone

Tuesday, May 20, 1975, dawned with a clear sky and a temperature of 60°F, portending a beautiful spring day in the woods now completely green and offering all the protection and sustenance a chipmunk could desire. Only the songs of the birds broke the silence of one of nature's finest hours. The young chipmunks had gone to seek their fortunes and the adults were left alone in the world of their feelings and perceptions, a particular world defined for them by their particular sensory apparatus and probably not very similar to our world.

A few moments before 6:00 a.m., sounds of digging and scratching in the earth were heard from Lady Cheltenham's burrow as she began opening the entrance she had so carefully closed the previous evening when she retired. This security measure was probably not taken in the false hope that it would prevent the entry of a blacksnake, a weasel, or even a rat into her sacred and well-concealed domain during the night, but rather so that the predator could not enter silently, giving her no time to defend herself, for despite the small size of her ears, her hearing is her most powerful and valuable sense.

Even though the importance of a chipmunk's hearing is obvious after even superficial observation for a period of time, two incidents confirm it dramatically. One day in the fall of 1978, I was observing Lady Cheltenham's burrow from a blind close by while monitoring with headphones the sound from a microphone mounted five inches over the entrance. Mistress Earwicker was situated at the entrance to her own burrow about fifteen feet away and completely out of sight of her mother's entrance. Consistently, over a period of almost two hours, sounds from Lady Cheltenham's burrow that were barely detected by the microphone drew Mistress Earwicker's attention unquestionably toward the area of her mother's burrow.

During the summer of 1977, Gutrune spent half a day carrying sunflower seeds from the back porch to her burrow thirty feet away. On one of her journeys she carried her goods into the burrow and emerged about two minutes later. During the two minutes she was underground, a gray squirrel appeared from the woods, buried two hickory nuts under a bush about six feet from her entrance and disappeared. The instant she emerged, Gutrune made a beeline to the bush, dug up the hickory nuts and carried them home. In both cases, sensitive hearing, perhaps even enhanced by tactile sensitivity to ground vibrations, produced striking events.

Gradually, the scratching sounds from the burrow subsided and were followed by five minutes of silence as Lady Cheltenham waited patiently in her entrance just below the surface, listening attentively. Ever since her first introduction to the world from a similar burrow she had listened, becoming habituated to the normal sounds of the woods—to the birds singing, the leaves rustling in the wind, a branch falling, the hopping footsteps of a rabbit, the background noise of nature. What she did not want to hear was silence, for if the birds were quiet and if there had been no sense of motion in the woods, that would have indicated the presence of a strangeness, perhaps a predator, something she understood, or worse yet, something she did not understand.

Having heard nothing, since the normal sounds of the woods were a kind of silence to her, Lady Cheltenham raised her head above the surface, looking toward open ground. Confident that nothing could sneak up on her from the brush behind without detection by her sensitive ears, she examined the open lawn with her less sensitive eyes. Probably able to see over a

Figure 36. Lady Cheltenham examines her domain.

range of about 270°, 90° binocularly or with both eyes at once; possibly able to see in color, since some other ground and tree squirrels have eyes adapted to color vision; and probably only able to see indistinctly at a distance; she was looking for movement. Not the movement of the grass in the wind, or of the birds, a squirrel, a rabbit, but rather she looked for an unfamiliar movement, one that was out of place in her world. Had she seen such a movement she would have disappeared back into the burrow in a flash.

The very indefinite description of her visual perception reflects our honesty in admitting that we cannot get inside the heads of chipmunks and see through their eyes or hear through their ears. We can only guess at what they see or hear from observing their behavior in relation to what *we* see or hear, which may be something entirely different.

The insecurity of their vision is frequently shown in their behavior, particularly by their difficulty in locating dropped objects or even each other in the grass. A pursued chipmunk will often simply stop and remain frozen in the grass. The pursuer is likely to depart disappointed at not

having been able to locate its quarry even after searching within a few inches of the target. An acorn dropped in the grass during a fight is almost never found afterward, but is usually discovered by someone else accidentally.

Their inability to locate one another under these circumstances would also seem to indicate a poorly developed sense of smell, an uncommon feature in rodents and especially in other squirrels. So if we do not see Lady Cheltenham's nose wrinkle up and move like a rabbit's, we should not be surprised, even though her rapid breathing, frequently mistaken for heartbeat, seems to indicate some reliance on the sense of smell.

Both John Burroughs and Elsa Allen reported that chipmunks are not able to locate hidden nuts in the way that gray squirrels do. Others have attributed the unerring accuracy with which chipmunks pounce on nuts thrown in the grass to their sense of smell, but it is more likely that their sensitive ears hear the impact with the ground. Although chipmunks frequently appear to mark territorial areas with urine and feces, and although they possess rudimentary anal scent glands, their chemical communication appears to be confined pri-

Figure 37. Gutrune emerges cautiously from her burrow.

marily to the male's detection of estrous females.

Having satisfied herself that there was no recognizable movement on the lawn, Lady Cheltenham climbed out of the entrance, sat upright with her front paws clasped to her breast (fig. 36), and proceeded to examine the totality of her world, gazing and listening in every direction, a picture of the alertness that characterizes a chipmunk.

What was she thinking? Now, several years ago that would have been considered a naughty question for a naturalist to ask. In fact, many still consider it a foolish question, for doesn't everyone know that only humans think? Of course, but humans once thought that the earth was the center of the solar system, too. Do chipmunks enjoy mental experiences, properties of the mind that allow them to consider things and events that are remote from their presence? Do they enjoy that quality of awareness that allows them to entertain mental images of a progression of events? Can they have intentions, mental images in which they picture themselves as participants and choose whether or not to convert them to reality? Do they possess consciousness, the sum of all of these questions?

I am personally grateful to Donald Griffin, the first naturalist of unchallenged reputation to answer these questions in his re-

markable book *The Question of Animal Awareness.* His answer: why not? After exposing the problem in detail, he states on p. 101:

> The hypothesis that some animals are indeed aware of what they do, and of internal images that affect their behavior, simplifies our view of the universe by removing the need to maintain an unparsimonius assumption that our species is qualitatively unique in this important attribute.

Then he concludes on p. 104:

> The possibility that animals have mental experiences is often dismissed as anthropomorphic because it is held to imply that other species have the same mental experiences a man might have under comparable circumstances. But this widespread view itself contains the questionable assumption that human mental experiences are the only kind that can conceivably exist. This belief that mental experiences are a unique attribute of a single species is not only unparsimonius; it is conceited. It seems more likely than not that mental experiences, like many other characters, are widespread, at least among multicellular animals, but differ greatly in nature and complexity.

The last statement that the experiences "differ greatly in nature and complexity" is the key to the whole problem. Since no one has come up with a method for objectively studying these experiences, perhaps if we ignore them they will go away. It then takes only a small act of faith to believe that they do not exist. This act of faith can be seen to be a recent development in behavioral science if we remember that Charles Darwin assumed that animals had not only mental experiences but emotions as well.

What was Lady Cheltenham thinking as she stood, duckpinlike, studying her world? I really cannot know, nor can anyone, but I think it would not be outrageous to keep the possibility of her thoughts in mind

Figures 38 and 39. Fenwick climbs to greater heights; Guinevere descends.

as we examine her behavior during the remainder of this chapter.

Convinced by 6:15 that her world was in order, Lady Cheltenham relaxed and moved slowly to a hickory tree fifteen feet south of her entrance, scampered to a branch about six feet above the ground, and began her morning song. She chipped regularly at a rate of 110 chips per minute for approximately ten minutes. Her typical, high-pitched song could be heard 600 feet away. What was she saying, or rather, singing? As we shall see, the motivation for the chipmunk's spontaneous song has never been explained. Perhaps she was saying, "I feel chip-chip this morning."

Having notified the world of the state of her existence, she stretched herself luxuriously in a gesture of purely decadent relaxation. Grasping the trunk of the tree with her hind feet, she extended her front legs fully downward and outward, while arching her back to its fullest extent away from the tree, hanging there for several seconds with every muscle stretched to the breaking point. Then she descended the tree and returned to her burrow entrance, where she began her morning bath. Using teeth, tongue, and claws, she scoured every part of her body. She washed behind her ears, but neglected to dry between her toes. In less than three minutes she was perfect. Cleanliness activity is not, however, confined to the morning bath, but reappears periodically throughout the day. It appears to be an attitude rather than a task, and is no doubt necessary to her avoidance of predators.

Chipmunks are able to reach every part of their bodies. The face and neck are washed by moistening the forepaws with saliva and then rubbing briskly. The tail is groomed in a truly unique way by taking advantage of the space between the incisors and the premolars. The jaws grasp the tail firmly at its base and the head moves upward in a sweeping gesture that causes the entire tail to move over tongue and teeth in a combined washing and brushing motion. The whole result was described by Burroughs: "...how well these wild creatures are groomed—every hair in its place and

Figures 40–43 (clockwise from top left). Chipmunks groom themselves periodically through-out the day. Here are three shots of Fenwick as he scrubs his leg, face, and tail (also see colorplate 11, page 74), and another of Guinevere, who is scratching herself vigorously.

shining as if it had just been polished. The tail of my chipmunk is simply perfect—not a hair missing or soiled or worn."

Because of their cleanliness, chipmunks are afflicted with few external parasites, according to Elsa Allen. Some individuals may harbor a flea or a mite or two, but on only rare occasions is a heavily infested animal encountered. The "bot" or "warble" (*Cuterebra emasculator*) is a fly that apparently lays eggs in the grass. The larvae, which are specific for chipmunks as hosts and which seem to be picked up during the chipmunk's normal activity, burrow under the skin of the abdomen where they continue their life cycle, and later emerge as adults. During their incubation within the host, they produce a large swelling which may become infected after the further developed larvae depart. Incubation occurs during August and September and supplies the origin of the curious specific name *emasculator*, for it was once believed that the larval infection destroyed the male chipmunk's testicles. Since it was later realized that the testicles disappear into the abdominal cavity during September anyway, the name is inappropriate.

Unless infested with three or more larvae, chipmunks appear to be little inconvenienced by this parasite, whose presence seems to be quite variable in both time and place. While Elsa Allen records it as uncommon in central New York, Lang Elliott reports 50 percent of the animals in his Adirondack study to have been infected. During the summers of 1974 through 1979 I had not observed a single case in Virginia, and when I was just about to propose its existence extremely rare or nonexistent this far south, three cases showed up in the late summer of 1980, all three in male chipmunks. One of them was Ipswich (fig. 44), who, I am happy to report, emerged from hibernation on February 18, 1981, in unemasculated breeding condition.

By 6:30, Lady Cheltenham was wide awake and squeaky-clean, ready for a day of adventure. She began foraging in her territory, moving slowly from place to place while examining the ground carefully. Occasionally, she stopped to taste a discovery, but never became too absorbed to come alert every three or four seconds for a look around. Often she became alert for several seconds or even a minute, looking attentively in the direction from which she may have thought she had seen a strange movement or heard a strange sound. Eventually, she approached the edge of the woods and encountered a bed of dry oak leaves. She picked one up with her teeth and, rising to her full duckpin height, neatly folded it against her breast with her forepaws, stuffed the compact bundle into her mouth, and carried it into her burrow to be shredded for bedding.

Strangely, I have noticed over the years that this leaf gathering seems to be a kind of synchronized behavior. A number of chipmunks may be active in the woods at a particular time doing various things. Suddenly they are all seen gathering leaves at once for several minutes as though a news broadcast had predicted an impending shortage. The behavior has been too consistent to be coincidence, but whatever mysterious signal calls up this response appears to be beyond our understanding.

Returning to Lady Cheltenham, she reappeared from her burrow within a minute

or so, and with much less caution than we observed earlier, and continued gathering leaves for five or ten minutes, by which time her mattress had apparently been fluffed up to comfortable proportions. She then went back to foraging, but farther from home.

During her previous activities, Lady Cheltenham had frequently paused and focused her attention on the back porch of the house about thirty feet away as though to decide if that strange bipedal creature who lived in the stone mountain with holes in its sides had provided the usual supply of sunflower seeds and if the other chipmunks were helping themselves. How could she, from her opportunistic point of view, possibly understand an animal giving away food? It probably never occurred to her to try to understand, but by 6:45 she was ready to help herself, too.

She scampered twenty-five feet south-west to the dogwood tree by the well, paused briefly on a low branch for a final examination of her destination, and dashed the last twenty-five feet west over a well-worn path to the porch. Yes, the others were helping themselves and competing ferociously for the sunflower seeds in the log pile and on the upturned logs that represented feeding tables. Her interaction with the others and their interaction with each other are the subjects of chapter 6, so to make a long story short, she spent the next

several hours in the competition, filling her cheek pouches and taking home load after load of sunflower seeds at a mad pace. She frequently made the thrushes on the lawn jump out of her way. Each time she took a load home, she would reappear from her entrance a minute later with little apparent caution, pause momentarily, wash her hands and face, and dash back to the porch. The inevitable face washing she probably felt was necessary because the distention of her filled cheeks caused them to rub against the sides of the entrance when she went down to unload. Indeed, sometimes she had difficulty fitting her swollen head into the door at all.

As her excitement and the competition increased, she began announcing her departure from her territory each time with a battle cry: "Chirrup, chip, chip, chip." I always interpreted this cry simply as a sign of exuberance rather than as a warning to her competitors because no one seemed to pay it any attention. If she thought she was saying, " Outta my way you bums, here comes the fiercest chipmunk in Spotsylvania County!" she would soon have given it up for lack of response.

Throughout her life Lady Cheltenham always used her battle cry when the fever of competition reached an intense level. The only other chipmunk with a battle cry was Willoughby, who may have been her son and who lived in a burrow close to hers. He may even have learned it from her.

Shortly before noon, the food supply had been exhausted and, living close by, Lady Cheltenham remained on the porch exploring the woodpile or just meditating on a log. She stretched out comfortably on the table or the top of the woodpile, and, with her paws crossed in front of her, stared silently into the woods for long periods of time. It is difficult to believe that she was not thinking about something in this beautifully meditative posture that lasted almost two undisturbed hours, for all of the others had gone home or to forage elsewhere. Suddenly she was on her feet and home into the burrow for an afternoon

Figure 46. Vladimir explores the mysterious.

Figure 47. Lady Cheltenham meditates. She would sometimes remain in this position for two hours or so.

siesta, a common practice during the heat of the day.

At 5:30 p.m., Lady Cheltenham reappeared from her burrow much as she had in the morning, but with not quite the caution of her earlier emergence. She came to the porch at once to see if the larder had been replenished, and was not disappointed. But the supply was more limited and the competition not as intense. After carrying her share home she again remained on the porch exploring. Suddenly she encountered something new. A microphone I had placed close to the floor to record the sounds coming from deep inside the woodpile was a new object in her limited world. As it always does, curiosity triumphed and she approached the strange oblong aluminum object cautiously, her tail swinging slowly from side to side in a rippling fashion.

As she slowly closed in, her hind feet suddenly would go no further and she stretched her body in order to bring her nose and whiskers in contact with the alien artifact. It was as though her hind feet, stamping alternately, said "no closer," but her exploratory instinct had to be satisfied. This is typical exploratory behavior and, having decided that the new object was not threatening, she went about her business examining the rest of the porch.

The manner in which she familiarizes herself with a new object is an example of ritualized behavior, a behavior that predicts a chipmunk's intentions or next move. The chipmunk's overall behavior is rich in these so-called intention movements, many of which can be seen in the illustrations throughout this book. The relaxed versus duckpin postures (figs. 36 and 5) are examples. The slight forward crouch or extended posture prior to movement (fig. 48) and the raising of one front paw as a sign of indecision as to whether to remain or flee (fig. 49) are two more examples. A wealth of these will be described in chapter 6 when we talk about social interaction. Other chipmunks always seem to know what behavior these postures predict even if we, as observers, learn only slowly. This is good evidence for a kind of consciousness on the part of the chipmunk, for if other chipmunks know what they mean as intentions, it would be foolish to imagine that the posing chipmunk did not know what it intended to do.

As dusk began to fall Lady Cheltenham began to think about going home. She seemed nervous. Whether her nervousness resulted from the growing darkness or from the anticipation of what was to come cannot be said, but she remained upright at the edge of the porch staring fixedly at the dogwood tree for five minutes. She made

Figures 48 and 49. *Gutrune ready to move (left); Gutrune indecisive.*

several false starts toward the tree, returning each time to the edge of the porch in order to examine her route again. She finally dashed madly toward the security of the tree and as she reached three-quarters of the way, a red-tailed hawk dropped like a stone out of the sky with her striped back in its sights.

Whether Lady Cheltenham's sensitive ears detected the rush of air through still feathers as the hawk spread its wings to break its fall, or her sense of survival acted in a very mysterious way, she changed direction at what seemed the instant of impact and escaped into a hole beneath the tree. No chipmunk travels without a complete knowledge of hiding places along the way. The hawk thrashed on the ground for several seconds, either looking for its lost dinner or trying to free its claws from their implantation in the ground, while Lady Cheltenham began singing a soft chucking song from her sanctuary.

Apparently unable to hear or to recognize the song, which was clearly audible to me thirty feet away, the hawk paid no attention and finally flew away mourning its lost culinary delicacy with a series of hoarse whistles. Ten minutes later, Lady Cheltenham ended her song and ran with truly inspired enthusiasm to her burrow. She was heard scratching and digging with extra zeal as she secured her home for the

night. So ended, on this melodramatic note, a typical early summer day in the life of a chipmunk.

Several times in the course of Lady Cheltenham's adventures I have mentioned her vocalization, and since language is frequently described as the distinctive feature of human intelligence, an examination of the chipmunk's vocal repertoire might lead to a better understanding of the differences between human consciousness, our only reference point, and chipmunk consciousness. We may assume from the outset that because the Eastern chipmunk is a solitary and fiercely independent creature, its need for communicating, especially vocally, is minimal. Much of the evidence seems to justify this assumption. Nevertheless, the chipmunk's vocal repertoire is both rich and fascinating.

Chipmunk vocalization has been observed to be a somewhat seasonal phenomenon. Those animals that remain active through the winter are generally silent except when extremely annoyed, which is rare. Possibly this silence occurs because few are active, but it also challenges the theory that the beginning of early spring activity can be dated by listening for chipmunk song. During the spring, vocalization becomes slightly more frequent as more animals become active. The full chorus does not enter until mid-April when young chip-

Colorplate 9. A youngster learns to negotiate three-dimensional space. Although young chipmunks begin climbing after the second or third day out of the burrow, their balance and self-confidence are not fully developed until dispersal time.

Figure 50. Guinevere delivers a campaign speech.

Figure 51. Mistress Earwicker scolds.

munks may be about, and it culminates during May when the epideictic vocalization (page 56) accompanying dispersal fills the woods with chipping.

During early and mid-summer, chipmunks are heard fairly frequently as they come into contact with one another and when they engage in spontaneous song. They quiet down after the July mating season (if there is one) only to begin their second epideictic vocalization in mid-September when a second crop of youngsters are dispersing. This seasonal pattern has been observed to some extent by many naturalists.

A catalog of the sounds produced by the Eastern chipmunk is described briefly in figure 52. Before we consider each of the six types of vocalization, the tabular headings need some explanation. "Song" refers to situations in which the chipmunk repeats the sound in a regular rhythm for a period of time. The maximum duration observed and the rates at which the sound is repeated are indicated. The heading "response to?" refers to the behavioral conditions during which the sound is produced.

"Semantic content" is the information delivered or the communicative value of the sound. In *Sociobiology*, Edward O. Wilson writes, "biological communication is the action on the part of one organism (or cell) that alters the probability pattern of behavior of another organism (or cell) in a fashion adaptive to either one or both of the participants." It is the relationship between a signal and a response.

Communication is so closely allied with consciousness that the same problems are projected by both, making it difficult to distinguish *intrinsic* and *semantic* messages. The intrinsic information in any vocalization is the information that is actually presented, whether or not the animal intends to present it. Lady Cheltenham's morning song contained the following intrinsic message: "I am a chipmunk, I am where I am." Possibly we could add: "I am the particular chipmunk that I am, age two seasons," or even, "I am Lady Chelten-

68

Figure 52. *Vocal repertoire of the Eastern Chipmunk.*

Sound	Song	Response To?	Semantic Meaning
Chip	>30 minutes 60-130 per minute	Surprise Spontaneous song Ground predator Epideictic vocalization	No No Maybe Probably not
Chuck	>30 minutes 60-130 per minute	Anger, annoyance Threat Hawk alarm	No Maybe Yes
Trill (chip, chuck)	—	Anger, exuberance, surprise, threat	No
Whistle	—	Mating chase (males)	Yes
Chatter (squeal, growl)	—	Anger, annoyance Mother and young	Maybe Maybe
Warble	Continuous	?	No

ham" rather than Gutrune, Fenwick, or someone else. Stretching the possible meaning further, it could even say: "My inner disposition or feeling today is chip-chip."

Where we may have crossed the line between intrinsic and semantic in this case is difficult to determine because no response was observed on the part of the other chipmunks. The semantic content of a message is the part that conveys what the animal intends to convey and is more closely related to what we normally think of when we consider human communication. I say normally, because human communication is loaded with intrinsic signals as well. Lady Cheltenham's battle cry may have had semantic meaning but, again, we observed no response to it.

This brings up another "consciousness" problem. We can only evaluate an animal's immediate response to a signal because we can only interpret its immediate behavior. We have no way of knowing whether or not a chipmunk can receive a message and, rather than responding to it at once, store

it in its memory for use in altering its behavior later on.

Another set of categories into which signals can be placed is that of discrete, or stereotyped, as opposed to graded. The former can say only "yes" or "no," while the latter can express gradations of contextual meaning or say "maybe." As we shall see, the chipmunk's vocal repertoire measures up to all of these distinctions, and each individual chipmunk shows a degree of variation with regard to how it expresses itself.

"Chip" is an onomatopoetic word that accurately describes the sound so named. If we were to look at a two-dimensional graphic representation of a single chip processed by a sound spectrograph, an instrument that transforms a sound signal into a plot of frequency, or pitch, versus time, we would see a downward sweep from 10 to 3 kiloherz (kHz) of about 0.05-second duration. For reference, the upper limit of human hearing lies between 15 and 20 kHz, the highest note on a piano has a fundamental frequency between 4 and 5 kHz, and

Colorplate 10. After several minutes of listening just below the surface, the chipmunk, satisfied that the world sounds normal, appears in the burrow entrance, looking cautiously for the absence of unfamiliar movement.

most of human speech lies between 100 Hz and 1,000 Hz or 1 kHz. It may be uttered as a loud chip, audible over a range of 600 feet, or anywhere down to a soft musical "chirp" that is barely audible even from close by.

The range of pitch is about the same for all adult chipmunks, but a bit higher in juveniles, making them easily distinguishable from adults even after they have achieved full growth. Occasionally, a chipmunk is heard chipping a little sharper (higher pitch) than usual for no obvious reason. Much less frequently a very sharp squeaky chip is heard.

The chip can be produced as a single sound, but as figure 52 shows, it usually appears in the form of a song continuing for anywhere between a few seconds and about thirty minutes. The rate depends upon the apparent state of excitement of the animal, increasing from about 60 to 130 chips per minute when excitement is at its peak. Chipmunks frequently sing this song for no apparent reason and when they do, it seems to be ignored by other chipmunks. Christopher Dunford reports that singing chipmunks are never approached, but I have found this not to be the case in Virginia. Even song produced within a chipmunk's own territory does not inhibit traffic through that territory, and, although this is infrequent, I have seen chipmunks attacked while singing on a feeding table.

Lady Cheltenham's morning song is a good example of this common vocalization, and its cause has never been explained. Perhaps it is a statement of loneliness. Being the solitary creatures that they are, while at the same time realizing that they must socialize on occasion in order to reproduce, maybe they simply need to make their presence known and hear others singing as assurance that this brief social contact will be available when the time comes.

Sometimes the song results from some disturbance obvious to the chipmunk, but a complete mystery to us. On one occasion during the summer of 1975, Lady Cheltenham suddenly stood upright on the edge of the porch and, looking intently towards a point in the woods, delivered a fifteen-minute sermon in her loudest and most rapid voice. I could detect nothing unusual nor could her companions, whose activity continued as usual.

In exasperation, I finally moved in and crouched down about eighteen inches behind her in order to see the woods from her perspective. I saw nothing, but so intently was she concentrating that she paid absolutely no attention to me, continuing her song with eyes glued on that point in the woods. After trying to distract her with small talk, I gave up and returned to the house. She gave up a few minutes later and went home. I admired her power of concentration, as well as her faith that as I stood behind her I was not preparing for dinner.

When we walk through the woods, on occasion we violate a chipmunk's elbow room and it departs quickly with a trill. It is common then for the indignant subject to reappear at some safe location and sing a rapidly composed song. This is the same response we get from gray squirrels, which like to sit on a safe tree limb and scold us in what is literally a vulgar tongue. I have seen domestic cats produce the same response in the woods. The song always comes from a safe distance behind the cat's route, never ahead of it. Other chipmunks in the immediate area become alert, but sixty feet away activity continues normally. The few times I have watched a red fox walk through the area there was only silence. Apparently foxes are considered professionals, in an entirely different class from soft, house-fed pussycats.

At dawn one summer morning I found a white house cat (with a bell attached to its collar) seated next to the entrance of Fenwick's burrow. It sat motionless for fifteen minutes, its eyes fixed on the entrance, waiting to pounce upon the emerging chipmunk for breakfast. Having complete faith in Fenwick's ingenuity, I refrained from interfering and ten minutes passed before it was light enough for me to notice Fenwick himself lying comfortably on a tree branch about ten feet from the cat's head with his eyes fixed on his uninvited guest.

The cat finally left and Fenwick went about his business, proving that you have to get up mighty early to fool a chipmunk. During the entire siege Fenwick had not made a sound nor blinked an eye. Nor had a tinkle been heard from the pussycat's bell.

The epideictic vocalization described in chapter 4 is the best-known example of the spontaneous chipping song. A genetic compulsion probably produces this behavior in which most of the available adults in the population sing continuously during the time the young are being dispersed. Its intrinsic message is clearly territorial and serves the several adaptive purposes already described, principally the regulation of population density. This display has a peculiar aspect to it that is not obvious unless considered carefully. Each chipmunk sings in its own rhythm, which is unaffected by the different rhythms of the others. Now, try beating a constant rhythm on a table when someone else in the room is beating a different one. This ability requires tremendous inward concentration and shows superb musicianship. I'll wager that, properly trained, a single chipmunk could play all of the percussion parts in Stravinsky's "Rite of Spring" without missing a note.

Examples of semantic meaning in the chipping song are difficult to come by. I present two situations and ask you to judge them. On September 13, 1975, Lady Cheltenham and Gutrune had been competing for food on the back porch during the early morning and Gutrune, the most vindictive of chipmunks, had taken every opportunity to give her competitor a hard time. At 8:30 Lady Cheltenham sat chipping at her entrance and Gutrune sat listening at hers about sixty feet away on the other side of the dogwood tree. On the final chip of her song, Lady Cheltenham catapulted toward the dogwood on her way to the porch. In a precisely synchronized movement and

without waiting to hear whether or not another chip or more song would follow, Gutrune started for the dogwood, where the two met with the ultimate precision and continued their battle. Was there a signal?

On May 6, 1975, at 8:00 a.m., Lady Cheltenham sat singing on a fallen branch about three feet behind her entrance where her four youngsters were playing. Suddenly, without even a slight alteration in the rhythm, the pitch dropped about one-quarter tone and instantly all four youngsters disappeared into the burrow. She continued her flat song for six more measures and then followed them. Three seconds later a rabbit walked slowly out of the woods and through the territory.

In order to assess the semantic content of various vocalizations, I conducted during the summer of 1977 several experiments in which recorded songs by one chipmunk were played to another chipmunk in a different area. The speaker was placed in a bush within the subject's area and a microphone was installed near the subject's burrow entrance so that I could hear as well as watch the response. The additional microphone also allowed me to judge how natural the recording sounded to the subject. All of these operations were engineered from inside the house. Two recordings were used: Lady Cheltenham's morning song and another she had sung at her entrance just after she had chased Launcelot out of her burrow. If anything, the latter had all the makings of a territorial statement and it was anticipated that if Gutrune, the subject, heard the song sung within her own territory, she might become a little upset.

The songs were played several days apart at times when Gutrune was just hanging around her entrance not doing much of anything. In both cases her attention was only momentarily attracted to the source of the sound. She remained in her original position and continued doing not much of anything. She either had nerves of steel, knew what I was up to, or simply was unconcerned. There was no evidence that she even resented the intrinsic message originating within her territory.

The "chuck," heard less frequently because it does not carry as far as the chip, is another onomatopoetic word. The sound spectrograph reveals a downward sweep from 3 to 1 kHz of about 0.02-second duration. A fortissimo chuck is about as loud as a pianissimo chip. It may be compared to a musical clucking sound and was described by Ernest Thompson Seton as sounding like a horse's hooves on a hard pavement. The sound was considered by Dunford as a lower pitched gradation of the chip, but I tend to agree with Elliott and A. P. S. Niedhardt that is a distinct sound in its own right.

As figure 52 shows, the chuck is delivered in much the same manner, at a similar rate and for similar durations, as the chipping song. It is also used more frequently as a single-syllable expression. The spontaneous chucking song is usually a result of nervousness or some annoyance shortly past, and it may continue intermittently during the activity that follows. It is delivered with considerably more variation among individual chipmunks and I have actually become able to identify a few by their chucking voices. A common use of the chucking song is the hawk alarm, as the following incidents illustrate.

At about 3:30 p.m. on November 7, 1976, when the trees were almost bare but most of the chipmunks were still active, three chipmunks were feeding on the porch as a male marsh hawk glided across the lawn in his characteristic low-altitude reconnaissance. All three chipmunks dove into the woodpile simultaneously and one began a soft twenty-nine-minute chucking song. All activity ceased in the woods. As the vocalist's voice began to weaken, one of the others picked up the song and continued it for another ten minutes. During this forty-minute period only one chipmunk was seen moving in the woods as he stuck his head out of a stump after twenty-two minutes. Cautious movement resumed at the end of the song, but uninhibited activity was not restored until the original vocalist, probably the only one who had actually seen the hawk, became fully active and left the porch confidently.

Exactly one week later, at 4:00 p.m., a hawk dove into the woods like a meteor. It remained on the ground for about one minute, thrashing in the leaves before it left, apparently empty-clawed. There was no immediate alarm, but activity ceased in the entire area. At 4:10, two chipmunks were heard from the direction in which the hawk had departed. Four chipmunks on the porch did not hide, but remained immobile. When the chucking duet ended at 4:20, they all scattered for home. Fenwick, who was in an exposed position atop a stone structure about thirty feet away, remained motionless in position until 4:30.

Two days later at about 7:10 a.m., a redtailed hawk flew silently into the woods from the north and landed on a tree limb about thirty feet from the ground. Its arrival was unnoticed, but when it flew east about a minute later, its wing beats resounded through the woods like thunder. Chipmunks that had been in the open froze in their tracks and some that had been concealed actually came into the open and froze. Several were heard chucking for about five minutes, after which normal activity resumed. Apparently none of them had actually seen the hawk. At about noon on September 1, 1980, I was able to record both cause and effect for the first time: a chorus of chucking accompanied musically by the cries of a Cooper's or sharp-shinned hawk. Chipmunk activity ceased for about thirty minutes.

The story of Lady Cheltenham's hawk adventure has already been told. A similar incident occurred on April 8, 1977. Willoughby and Rinaldo had been fighting all day over their territorial boundaries and the food supply. As the excitement mounted, Willoughby began delivering a battle cry similar to Lady Cheltenham's each time he left his area. In both cases, the use of the battle cry may have invited trouble, for at 5:45, just as Willoughby

Colorplate 11 (above). Fenwick completes the grooming of his tail with a flourish of elegance. His jaws grasp the tail firmly at its base and his head moves upward in a sweeping arc that draws the tail through the space between his incisors and premolars and over his tongue. Figure 43 shows an earlier stage in this action.

Colorplate 12 (opposite). "I am Juliana and I am standing right here!" The intrinsic message of this vocalization is clear as Jellicle's operatic daughter sings her song of exuberance and expressiveness. The chipmunk's vocal repertoire is varied and complex, but sometimes she sings just for the fun of it.

began the last leg of a journey through dense brush to his burrow, a male marsh hawk struck from a low angle behind. I did not see by what devious maneuver Willoughby escaped, but he ended up chucking softly in a hollow stump nearby, where he remained for ten minutes before dashing home to consider whether or not Rinaldo had bought a contract on him. As in the incident with Lady Cheltenham, the hawk thrashed about for a minute before flying off, having ignored or not heard Willoughby's song.

Elliott reviews and criticizes the hawk alarm as a case of altruism whereby, for the benefit of the community, one chipmunk may draw attention to itself by warning the others of danger. It appears from these and other similar observations, especially during 1976, when the hawk population seemed to be at a peak, that the chucking song does not expose the vocalist to increased danger, because hawks either do not hear it or have no idea of what it means. Possibly they do not even associate it with chipmunks or any other edible item. They may even have become habituated to a similar sound early in life. Therefore, it cannot be altruistic in any sense at all. In any case, there can be little doubt that the chucking song delivers some semantic information, at least in this context. It is a response to avian predators and never seems to accompany the presence of a surface predator.

Playback experiments confirmed what had been observed. When a recorded hawk-alarm chucking song was played to Gutrune, she fled to the safety of a tree trunk and remained crouched and alert for several minutes after the song ended. At the same time, another chipmunk on the porch thirty feet away froze. In a second trial, Lady Cheltenham fled into her burrow at once and did not reappear for several hours. The recording had been made by Fenwick, whom they probably both trusted as a hawk detector.

The chuck is used as a single syllable much more frequently than the chip, especially as a threat in aggressive interactions where individual chipmunks use many different variations. Hannibal, for example, when confronted by another chipmunk, always preceded his threat chuck with three rapid squeaks. This may have been a precise recognition feature, for Hannibal was always obeyed. Threats will be discussed further in chapter 6.

The category of trills, which includes squeals of all sorts, comprises some of the most variable elements in the chipmunk's repertoire. This trill consists of a rapidly delivered series of chips or chucks (occasionally both), sometimes at a rate of up to ten per second and almost appearing to be a single sound. The "chirrup" that precedes the three chips of Lady Cheltenham's battle cry is an example. Chip-trills of this type are heard commonly as we come upon a fleeing chipmunk in the woods or as one chipmunk is ambushed by another, especially in the wrong territory. A belligerent trill is executed by a proprietor chasing an invader from its territory, while the invader may utter a startled trill. Once heard, the difference is obvious. These so-called alarm squeals are common in the open woods, but are replaced by chuck-trills during face-to-face encounters at a feeding site. Here, of course, in close contact, attacks are anticipated and therefore are not so startling. Although they do not appear to alter behavior, trills do command a gesture of brief attention from those within hearing distance.

When chipmunks devote their full attention to some favorite project, they sometimes produce an intermittent series of soft musical trills that possess a fluttering quality. I once watched Willoughby acting very strangely in the brush behind Lady Cheltenham's burrow. He seemed to shuffle around suspiciously on the ground while producing these soft, fluttering trills. Then suddenly he would leap into the air and then return to his shuffling. I could not see exactly what he was doing and, when curiosity overcame me, an on-the-spot investigation revealed that he had been playing with a baby corn snake.

When Winthrop was courting Quail-feather in the spring of 1979, he remained at the entrance to her burrow for long periods of time singing flutter-trills to his intended. She did not respond. I have heard no other male engage in this seductive activity, possible because it does not seem to work. A recording of Lady Cheltenham's battle cry was played to several chipmunks in their own territories and produced no more than momentary attention.

What I have classified as chatter includes growls and prolonged squeals, heard when chipmunks are in very close contact. They may go unnoticed at a distance of a few feet, but are undoubtedly the most graded and variable sounds in the repertoire. Typical chatter is a gabbling sound, similar to

that of a gray squirrel but of much higher pitch and more rapidly executed. It almost sounds like a human voice played at a much faster speed than that at which it was recorded. It is frequently heard during aggressive encounters, during mating chases, and most often between a mother and her young. When a female chipmunk returns to her burrow entrance to find it stuffed with newly emerged youngsters, you may count on hearing a chatter conversation if you are close by. I cannot say whether or not any information is exchanged, but it seems to be an expression of displeasure—mama's to find the youngsters out of the burrow, the youngster's because they do not want to stay indoors.

The growl is an expression used only in very carefully controlled situations when a chipmunk is really furious. On three occasions during the spring and fall of 1976, Lady Cheltenham caught Launcelot in her burrow with her youngsters. She was not amused. During one of the incidents, a microphone was in place over her entrance and the whole ghastly scenario was recorded.

At 7:30 on the morning of October 6, Lady Cheltenham was peacefully foraging on her lawn when Launcelot, a scruffy male who lived nearby and who was the father of the litter that had emerged about a week earlier, slipped furtively out of the woods and into the burrow from which the youngsters had not yet appeared for the day. Lady Cheltenham seemed not to have noticed, but returned to the entrance a few seconds later and paused just below the surface. She remained in that position for almost two minutes delivering, every few seconds, a series of distinct growls of about one second duration. The sound had two syllables, "grrr-owl," with the first about a tone higher than the second (about B and A in the middle octave of a piano). I have no doubt that it had semantic meaning, but if it could be translated it would probably be unprintable. The sound literally seethed with rage.

After about two minutes of this monolog, chattering was heard approaching the sur-

Colorplate 13 (above). Fenwick enraged: the big bluff. When one chipmunk encounters another, intimidation is the name of the game. Every hair stands upright, the ears lie flat, the eyes are narrow slits. Every instinctive action contributes to the appearance of hugeness and ferocity. Maybe the other will run away and a dangerous fight will be avoided.

Colorplates 14 and 15 (opposite). The show of weapons. If the bluff fails, perhaps a threat will still avoid a fight. Lady Cheltenham finds Fenwick to be no gentleman (top) and decides that discretion is the better part of valor (bottom). The threat involves a show of teeth and is frequently accompanied by a vocal expletive.

face. I do not know whether this chatter came from the youngsters or from Launcelot, but he suddenly erupted from the entrance with Lady Cheltenham's teeth firmly attached to his right hind leg. They disappeared into the woods in a violent chase from which Lady Cheltenham returned in about thirty seconds. She entered the burrow for another thirty seconds and upon reappearing, chipped violently for fifteen minutes. It was this song that was used in the playback experiments because it seemed to be sung in such an obviously territorial context.

We cannot say exactly what happened inside the burrow because we only heard the action, but one possibility was that her growls were instructing the youngsters to gang up on Launcelot and chase him into her waiting jaws. In any case, he walked on three legs for a week afterward and was not seen visiting his children again.

The mating whistle has been described in chapter 3. It is a high-pitched, prolonged whistle apparently produced only by males during mating chases. On one occasion, I recorded it when Fenwick and Launcelot left a mating chase long enough to chase each other. Its function in mate selection by the female justifies its intrinsic and, possibly, semantic meanings.

The last sound listed in figure 52, the warble, is one that I have heard from Jellicle's daughter Juliana, and only once. I don't think I could have listened for six years without having heard it if it is at all common. I have not heard it since. It is a very soft, continuous warbling sound much like a high-pitched version of a cat's purr. On August 16, 1980, Juliana produced it continuously while foraging on the porch. It became louder as she moved closer to the microphone and seemed to change in phrasing and intensity with the rhythm of her movements. I have no idea of what it represented and it seemed to produce no reaction on the part of the other chipmunks.

How does the Eastern chipmunk's vocal repertoire compare with those of similar animals? The Uinta ground squirrel, *Sper-*

mophilus armatus, Belding's ground squirrel, *S. beldingi*, the California ground squirrel, *S. beecheyi*, and several species of Western chipmunks, *Eutamias*, have been examined and shown to have similar, but more complex, repertoires. For example, the Uinta ground squirrel chirps, churrs, squeals, squawks, growls, and clatters its teeth with remarkable efficiency, while the California ground squirrel gives three distinctly separate alarm calls for aerial predators, mammalian predators, and snakes. Their more complex vocalization and the fact that some seem to bark like dogs probably is appropriate to their social nature since they are less solitary than chipmunks.

Ten species of Western chipmunks found in California all chip, trill, chuck, chatter, chipper, growl, squeal, warble, and whistle. Those sounds bear a nominal resemblance to the ones I have described for the Eastern chipmunk, but all differ somewhat in structure, variability, and occasion for delivery by Western chipmunks as opposed to their eastern cousins. Western chipmunks overlap considerably in their ranges and therefore may require more sophisticated vocalization for mating recognition. Eastern chipmunks, all belonging to one species, know that any chipmunk around is likely to be of their own kind and suitable for a mate.

Let us conclude this chapter devoted to the inner self of the chipmunk by considering some familiar examples of its behavior, classified into three categories: purely instinctive, behavior requiring an awareness of time, and behavior requiring an awareness of space. Then we will take a brief look at its intelligence and learning ability.

Among purely instinctive or genetically programmed behaviors characteristic of the chipmunk we may obviously include food hoarding, because of its anthropomorphically obsessive dimension, and the epideictic vocalization during dispersal. No thought need be given to either by the animal. A less well-known example, described in chapter 4, is the chipmunk's

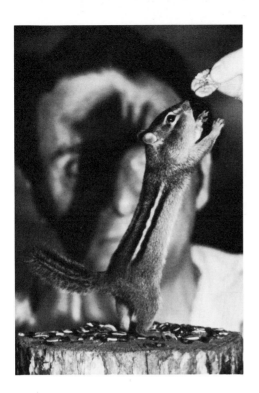

Figure 55. *Lady Cheltenham reaches for a pecan. "Let go—unless you have no further use for those fingers."*

reticence to enter its burrow while watched. We have no evidence that this is learned, and its selective value is obvious in protecting the secrecy of the home. Whether or not we are justified in including opportunism in this category is unclear.

A good example of opportunism is the tremendous population of chipmunks (uncaged) at the National Zoo in Washington. These chipmunks patrol the areas between the guard rails and the cages, picking up misplaced peanuts. I have even seen them enter the monkey cages to steal food, and on one occasion I watched a chipmunk enter an outdoor cage, occupied by a black panther, in order to pick up peanuts that a disillusioned child had expected the cat to eat. The great cat watched from its shelf, half asleep and unconcerned, since the chipmunk would have represented only the equivalent of half a peanut in its diet.

The chipmunk's awareness of time is demonstrated by its willingness to hide food for later recovery and storage. If it has a storehouse, it never seems to forget. Intention movements, although of almost immediate significance, show the consideration of future activities. Familiarity with particular humans is remembered from season to season. Visitors to public camp grounds and summer homes report this ability, and

it has been confirmed in the present study. Once Lady Cheltenham had learned that it was safe to climb into my hand for food, she never forgot. On the day she emerged from hibernation each spring she was nibbling at my fingers.

If we place ourselves in the position of a chipmunk, the world would appear very strange. The relationship between its size and that of the objects in its and our environment would present a very different picture than ours. In view of this, the chipmunk's awareness of space is truly remarkable. Its ability to navigate freely through the dense woods and over open spaces in its home range must imply the possession of a kind of mental map. Its awareness of places to hide along its routes implies a very significant capacity for spatial memory. Remember, no self-respecting chipmunk is ever caught without a convenient place to hide.

The chipmunk's homing ability, while modest in terms of our size, is quite impressive in terms of its size. Elsa Allen and James N. Layne have both reported the chipmunk's ability to find its way home when displaced up to 1,000 feet. Converted to human dimensions on the basis of relative body weight, this would represent 400 miles! More realistically, on the basis of relative height, it would represent five or six miles. The conclusion that chipmunks possess an awareness of events and things remote in time and space should be no surprise.

Chipmunks are generally believed to be smarter than gray squirrels, which spend the summer hiding nuts so they can spend the winter looking for them, and not as smart as red squirrels, which are more territorial and intraspecifically social. Of course, these involve survival strategies rather than intelligence. The only evidence we have of learning ability is the opportunistic nature of chipmunks and their ability to recognize nonthreatening humans. The latter behavior is contrary to instinct, which tells them to trust no one. Their curiosity is, however, their downfall.

They cannot seem to stay out of traps, even unbaited ones. Allen tells of a trap left unbaited in a large open cage that caught seven of the eight resident chipmunks. One was trampled to death by the crowd.

On the other hand, their ability to discriminate between perishable and non-perishable food for storage purposes may indicate a distinct degree of intelligence. It is impossible to determine whether or not a mother chipmunk teaches anything to her young because of the secrecy of the first six weeks of life in the burrow, but there is no evidence of teaching after emergence. Some mothers ignore their youngsters completely above ground.

I hope that this chapter has revealed some insight into the mind of the chipmunk. We left Lady Cheltenham to her thoughts in her doubly secured burrow after a hairbreadth escape. In the next chapter we shall see how she interacts with her companions.

6

Gutrune and Hannibal: Social Interaction

Following the dispersal of her four young-sters and a day or two devoted to reflection on the tranquility, or perhaps even the loneliness, of a solitary and independent existence, Lady Cheltenham returned to the discipline of her food-hoarding instinct and began to replenish the storehouse that had been ravaged by adolescent appetites. Her foraging brought her repeatedly to the back porch, which had by this time become a central feeding site for many chipmunks.

Elliott described a maple tree outside the boundaries of his study area which, when it shed seeds, attracted chipmunks from a wide region and allowed him, so long as the seeds lasted, to make some observations on their social behavior away from home. The back porch had, in a sense, become the permanent equivalent of Elliott's maple tree, with the additional advantages of close observation and the possibility of spreading or concentrating the food so as to require the chipmunks to interact with varying degrees of intimacy.

What Lady Cheltenham found, in addition to sunflower seeds, was that Fenwick still seemed to control the area—and indeed to be rather a bully everywhere—but that he was being challenged by Gutrune, the four-ounce female who had moved into Guilford's burrow in March. So powerful has her challenge and so well developed was her aggressive personality that, by late June, she had completely dis-placed his authority and tended to bully everyone indiscriminately. She even chased birds and gray squirrels out of her territory. Lady Cheltenham avoided her.

Having been introduced to the kinds of social behavior that occur during mating and the raising of young, we must now turn to the everyday social behavior that results from chance encounters and requires us to consider aggression with all of its Freudian connotations. It must be obvious by now that chipmunks do not suffer one another

graciously, and this is seldom more evident than when they are competing for food in close contact. Each chance encounter is an aggressive interaction that results from a conflict among motivations arising out of what Konrad Lorenz has labeled the great parliament of instincts. The principal dele-gates to this parliament are hunger, love, fight, and flight. In a solitary animal like the chipmunk, aggressiveness pays off be-cause it increases the animal's fitness by allowing it to control a greater share of the available resources: food, space, and mates.

If there is an optimal level of aggressive-ness above which fitness may be reduced, chipmunks seem to have found it. It has been shown that, although aggression is a common feature of intraspecific competi-tion, one animal is not often killed by another of the same species (Lorenz) for the simple reason that sometimes complicated, but always effective, mechanisms have evolved that enable contests to be settled in a less deadly manner.

As Richard Dawkins has pointed out so ruthlessly, if you kill a competitor, some-one else who is also a competitor may benefit more than you do. Settling argu-ments short of murder has obvious benefits in terms of the fitness of the individual, for the killer always runs the risk of being killed— and not being killed lengthens its life. Furthermore, the more ritualistic the settlement, the less risk there is of injury and the more time and energy both partici-pants conserve for more productive pursuits, such as mating and eating. The typical con-frontational behavior of the Eastern chip-munk exemplifies these principles.

When two chipmunks, under no special circumstances, find themselves too close for comfort and neither is in what might be called its own territory, the following sequence of events is usually observed. The first stage of the encounter is sometimes referred to as freezing and fixation (fig. 58),

and may last from one-half to ten seconds. Both contestants freeze, bodies close to the ground, eyes fixed upon one another in what appears to be a passive bluff. The objective is intimidation. Colorplate 13, page 78, shows a truly enraged chipmunk using every deceit at his diposal—ears close to head, eyes narrowed, every hair on his body erect—in order to appear large and formidable. One is reminded of Shakespeare's account of Henry V's advice to his soldiers before the siege of Harfleur (Act 3, Scene 1):

> . . . when the blast of war blows in our
> ears,
> Then imitate the action of the tiger;
> Stiffen the sinews, summon up the blood,
> Disguise fair nature with hard favour'd
> rage;
> Then lend the eye a terrible aspect;
> Let it pry through the portage of the head
> Like the brass cannon; let the brow
> o'erwhelm it
> As fearfully as. . . .

Frequently, one contestant withdraws and the confrontation ends peacefully. Occasionally, the passive victor pursues for a distance of five or ten feet as a gesture of authority. If the bluff is not successful, then one contestant must execute a visual or audible threat. A single chuck or a chuck-trill is accompanied by opening the mouth wide to expose the weapons of war. Figure 59 and colorplates 14 and 15 (page 79) demonstrate successful threats and bring us back to King Harry's advice:

> Now set the teeth and stretch the nostril
> wide;
> Hold hard the breath and bend up every
> spirit
> To his full height!—On, on you noble
> [Chipmunk]. . . .

Usually, one contestant withdraws at this point and the confrontation ends with at least some conservation of the peace. A chase following withdrawal is more common after a threat has been executed, but seldom extends for more than fifteen or twenty feet and almost never produces further combat.

If the threat is unsuccessful and the threatened party does not withdraw, it is necessary for the more aggressive of the two to attack. I have never seen a chipmunk back down after threatening another. The attack consists of a lunging bite directed usually toward the neck or upper back. There is still hope at this stage of the encounter for a modestly peaceful resolution if the attacked chipmunk executes a

Figure 58. Freezing and fixation: Lady Cheltenham (below) and Fenwick.

Figure 59. Hannibal disposes of White-Ears with a gesture.

precisely timed escape leap, as shown in colorplate 16, page 98. In this illustration we see Lady Cheltenham in the air avoiding Don Diego's attack. Seconds earlier, Don Diego had been feeding on the upturned log when he was displaced by Lady Cheltenham. With cheek pouches still filled, he returned immediately to the attack and was avoided by a leap into the air followed by a somersault that propelled Lady Cheltenham through six feet of space to the floor of the porch. She hit the ground running.

Should the attacked chipmunk elect to stand its ground, it may receive the attacker's bite (fig. 60), avoid it with a parry, or return a bite of its own. What results is a so-called roll-tumble fight (colorplate 17, page 99) in which the combatants wrestle together, biting and scratching for all they are worth. Lasting from a fraction of a second to about two seconds, the battle is ended when one kicks violently with its hind feet, twists free, and escapes.

Although the action is often too swift for accurate visual observation, neither eye nor camera has detected anything like a submissive or appeasement gesture common in more social animals. The loser realizes its mistake quickly and simply runs away. Furthermore, the common inhibition observed in males of more social species with

respect to attacking females does not exist in the Eastern chipmunk.

The roll-tumble fight is almost invariably followed by a fairly extensive chase during which the victor sometimes overtakes the loser with a resumption of brief combat, but with no murderous intent or permanent injury. The most reasonable explanation for the victor not trying to kill its weaker opponent would appear, from the selfish point of view, to be that the final act of killing would accomplish no further purpose than to utilize more energy and time, and would subject the victor to the danger of injury from the well-known ferocity of a desperate animal. Such behavior would not increase selective fitness. But such is the fury of the battle that the chase sometimes extends well into the home territory of the loser as much as fifteen to seventy-five feet away. When this happens we see a curious turn of events. Suddenly the pursued turns and becomes pursuer and the roles are completely reversed.

The concept of territoriality was mentioned earlier, but the true nature of a chipmunk's territory only becomes evident when we watch them chase one another. In chapter 2 the territory was defined as the area around the entrance to the burrow

Figure 60. Gutrune's teeth find Launcelot's flank.

within which a chipmunk can always be wagered upon to win a fight. Such is the security of home to a sedentary animal. Why then should the loser of a fight continue to be chased when it reaches its territory? It shouldn't and it isn't. The point at which the pursued turns pursuer is the territorial boundary and varies by no more than a few inches from day to day.

It must be remembered that while the pursued is approaching its territory and acquiring security, the pursuer is moving away from its territory and is becoming less secure. As the roles reverse, the chase moves toward the territory of the newly pursued and the opposite loss and gain of security occur until the latter reaches its territory and turns pursuer once more. Sometimes chases of this sort go back and forth several times. Should the chipmunks overtake one another in the area between their territories, a fair fight can ensue, but within territories, the proprietor is supreme.

This kind of partial territoriality has selective value in protecting food stores and the young. Females can be seen, for these reasons, to be much more ferocious defenders of their territories than males are of theirs. In terms of evolutionary strategies, the concept attributed to W. D. Hamilton and R. MacArthur by John Maynard Smith predicts that the game of "resident fights: intruder flees" is obviously a stable one. The outcome of almost any encounter can be predicted with relative accuracy by

noting the distances between the location of the fight and the territories of the fighters. Elliott has provided a mathematical equation for such predictions and it usually works.

Occasionally, there are exceptions to the ritualized behavior just described. When Hannibal, the conqueror from the south, visited the porch briefly in July 1975 (without his elephants), he was the essential gentleman who tolerated the presence of the others as long as they stayed out of his way. His encounters with Lady Cheltenham led to the invention of the Chipmunk Polka. After facing one another frozen for a few seconds, Hannibal would lunge at Lady Cheltenham without the usual truculent threat. She would then avoid his attack with a perfectly timed little jump, sometimes leaping completely over his back. This acrobatic dance would be repeated several times until both seemingly tired of it and went about their business.

Gutrune, the most ferocious of the lot, showed another peculiar pattern in her aggressiveness. On one occasion, a youngster minding its own business in Lady Cheltenham's area was the target of a thirty-foot charge by Gutrune from her own territory. As Gutrune approached, with what could have been interpreted as murderous intent, the youngster simply sat upright staring at her. At the final instant, Gutrune aborted her attack by jumping completely over her target.

Many times Gutrune leveled charging attacks on Lady Cheltenham from behind in neutral territory only to stop about three feet short of violence when her target turned and saw her. She seemed to attack her companions from behind, but always confronted strangers. It would seem more logical for her to think that she could bluff her companions who knew her strength and disposition.

On only two occasions did I see a chipmunk defeated in its own territory. In November 1976 Launcelot, a full-grown male of rather questionable reputation, ambushed Mistress Earwicker as she

Figure 61. Hannibal the Conqueror.

returned to her burrow from foraging. After a terrible roll-tumble fight, Mistress Earwicker, who was only three months old and considerably smaller than her barbaric attacker, escaped into her burrow. After taking a few seconds to collect her wits, she emerged and chased Launcelot thoroughly out of her territory with no difficulty at all. The other occasion, to be described later, involved two males in a mating season tournament.

In chapter 5 we described Willoughby's encounter with a hawk after a day of squabbling with Rinaldo. Just before he was almost eaten, Willoughby was leaving the porch, his cheek pouches filled to capacity, when Rinaldo appeared and attacked him repeatedly. Willoughby turned away, trying to keep Rinaldo behind him, and refused to fight back.

Finally, in exasperation, he emptied his cheek pouches on the lawn and returned Rinaldo's fire with several roll-tumble battles lasting a total of three or four minutes. Rinaldo finally fled, was pursued relentlessly and caught several times, all the way home to his burrow. Willoughby then retrieved his discarded provisions and went on to encounter the hawk.

With all their apparent savage ferocity, these combats seldom produce serious injury. In fact, I can only recount three instances during the entire six years of observation, if we exclude the numerous relatively benign tail-shortenings described in chapter 3. The possibility that Guilford's death may have resulted from a punctured cheek pouch that became infected, and Lady Cheltenham's crippling attack on Launcelot when she caught him molesting her children, have already been discussed. During the spring of 1980, Brunhilde fought with an unidentified female and was severely bitten on her right flank and left ear. She survived the event and went on to bear proudly the scar shown in colorplate 18 (page 102).

While severe injury is rare, the daily fights take their toll on a chipmunk's usually well-groomed appearance. Color plate 19 (page 102) shows Gutrune just before she molted in June 1975, when she had all but completed her conquest of the area.

At feeding sites remote from their territories, like the back porch and Elliott's maple tree, chipmunks generally avoid excessive energy waste from fighting by establishing a kind of dominance order, a relationship similar to the familiar pecking order among chickens but not so compellingly adhered to. This behavior is also reflected in their interactions in neutral territories within the home range.

In a true dominance order each animal knows its place and seldom challenges its superiors. Each benefits by having more time to do useful things rather than fighting or being injured. The animal at the top, of course, receives the most benefit and the entire system depends upon the animals being able to recognize one another. True dominance orders exist only among more social species, but when solitary chipmunks are forced into close contact within about three feet, they at least make an attempt at it.

It is evident that a true order does not exist, however, for it is not possible to distinguish dominant from subordinate chipmunks by their normal behavior. One must observe the outcomes of many aggressive encounters. Dominant chipmunks do not swagger, they mind their own business. Subordinate chipmunks do not crawl, they avoid dominant ones. But, then, a true dominance hierarchy is not adaptive for chipmunks since they do not live as a social unit, but simply respect one another's aggressiveness during somewhat infrequent encounters.

Studies have shown, however, that a dominance hierarchy may be adaptive in captive populations where death and injury can result from the inability of the loser to escape. Both Dunford and Elliott have observed the so-called spatial theory of dominance, which ranks the animals in order of their distance from home. The same phenomenon was observed in this study and described with respect to territoriality. Although relative size, age, and inherent aggressiveness also play important roles, they do not become exclusive determinants unless all members of the group are more than a hundred feet from home.

There are, however, some additional factors. Females seem to be generally more aggressive than males, presumably because they have more to protect in that they raise the young exclusively and therefore need a larger hoarded food supply. Aggressiveness increases in both males and females during the mating seasons. The increase in males seems to be related to testicular development and probably to the levels of androgenic hormones. Logically, then, testicular retraction during late spring and early summer would be selected for the protection of the emerging and dispersing young from male aggression. Female aggression seems greatest during lactation and the period of the emergence of the young, when they require protection. More detailed endocrine relationships will be considered in chapter 7. B. T. Aniskowicz and J. Vaillancourt and Richard A. Yahner have studied the aggressive behavior of wild chipmunks and have categorized several components of predictive value.

The dominance order in the local population has had a somewhat delicate structure. At times one chipmunk has been the un-contested bully while at other times the authority has been shared. When a female has been dominant, both sexes have tended to respect her authority, but when males have dominated, the females have tended to take them less seriously.

Lady Cheltenham was the unquestioned leader between November 1974 and February 1975, when she retired during her pregnancy and never completely regained her heroic stature. Fenwick ruled the area with almost complete authority between February and May 1975, until Gutrune displaced him. So well displaced was Fenwick by Gutrune's fierceness that in the fall of 1976 he could no longer tolerate living next door to her and moved his quarters about forty-five feet into the woods.

With the exception of two brief periods during which she bowed to Hannibal, Gutrune remained the unchallenged despot until her death in July 1977. Lady Cheltenham then regained some of her power and, in spite of arthritis, managed to dominate the group until her death in February 1978, although she was frequently challenged by Guinevere, Gutrune's daughter, and by Mistress Earwicker, her own daughter.

After Lady Cheltenham's death there appeared no clear case of despotic dominance. During 1978, Don Diego and Ipswich ruled almost equally until the former's disappearance in late summer. At this point Mistress Earwicker seemed to take over. During 1979, Ipswich and Bohort shared authority with Mistress Squatter, who was finally displaced by Mistress Earwicker shortly before her death in July. During 1980, Wallenstein, Clorindas, Winthrop, and Ipswich shared control along with Brunhilde, Tamora, and Juliana. No one was obviously dominant and the apparent hierarchy changed from day to day. It is evident that Eastern chipmunks recognize the strength and aggressiveness of their companions, but do not take the matter too seriously.

The Eastern chipmunk's aggressive attitude toward other species is one of tolerance, probably because its food-storage habits make its dependence on and competition for food resources less critical. Although gray squirrels frequently invade areas of concentrated food and act ruthlessly obnoxious toward chipmunks, the latter seem resigned to their size disadvantage and avoid belligerence. They sometimes use their swiftness, however, to swipe food literally from under the noses of their clumsy cousins, a practice that is greeted with much snapping and growling but with little retaliatory success.

Only once have I seen a chipmunk attack a squirrel and then with only modest truculence. Mistress Pellicle, Jellicle's daughter, had discovered a small pile of sunflower seeds on the front lawn and was busy transporting them home to her burrow forty-five feet away when a male gray squirrel made the same discovery. Not being a hoarder himself, he simply sat on the seeds and ate at his leisure.

When Mistress Pellicle returned from one of her trips home, she was quite upset. She circled him warily at a radius of about two feet and frequently lunged at him with a chuck-trill threat. He responded by remaining upright on the seeds and snapping back at her between mouthfuls. It almost seemed as though she was teasing him to chase her just to get him away from the seeds. She continued her teasing until he had finished his breakfast and left, whereupon she examined the remains without concealing her disappointment.

While chipmunks usually tolerate other species, they are not always treated with the same tolerance. I have recounted that Gutrune sometimes chased birds and squirrels out of her territory, but her threats may have been heeded because they had no compelling reason to be there in the first place.

On one occasion, Willoughby crossed the lawn north of his territory and explored the area along the fence. When he approached a cherry tree in which thrushes were nesting, he was attacked so viciously that he had to take refuge in the brush under the fence. Three times he tried to cross the lawn to get home, but each time he was forced to retreat under savage attack. I did not see him again that day and feared that he had been eaten, but he appeared in his own area on the following day none the worse for the experience. In desperation he must have followed the cover of the fence completely around the lawn in order to get back into the woods.

By early July 1975, Lady Cheltenham had developed the most sophisticated techniques for avoiding Gutrune, whose large size— she was a quarterpounder and a despotic bounder—and centrally located burrow only thirty feet from the porch combined with an outrageously aggressive personality to lend her virtually unchallenged authority over the area. She ruled with a firm hand, taking the best of food resources (she needed them), and extended her will to limit the territorial prerogatives of the others to an absolute minimum. As we have seen, she was also sneaky. For the remainder of her life, the only challenge to her authority occurred in the two-week mating seasons in late July of both 1975 and 1976, during which she completely folded under the persuasive influence of Hannibal. It might be said that he was the one love of her life.

Hannibal's burrow (no. 5) was located at the southern edge of the region about one hundred feet from the porch. When he began visiting Gutrune's area, his quiet strength was recognized at once by one and all and his authority was seldom questioned. Strangely, his aquisition of power seemed to be automatic, as he had little opportunity to demonstrate his martial abilities. The others stayed out of his way and were dismissed with the most brief and benign of threats. He was truly an exception to the spatial concept of dominance.

Hannibal's demeanor was gentle but firm. Only once did he pursue another chipmunk and then only for ten or fifteen feet after an unidentified transient female had the gall to challenge him at the feeding table four times in as many minutes. He generally made his will known with a characteristic chuck-trill, preceded by three squeaks, that brought about the immediate withdrawal of competitors. The transient female was, no doubt, unfamiliar with his regional dialect.

As the females began coming into heat and the period of active mating approached, Hannibal, in typical fashion, extended his operations to gain control of as many female territories as possible. Naturally, this brought him into close contact with the other males, who had the same idea, and his jousting talent was put to the test. Male mating season tournaments, mentioned in chapter 3, demonstrate the ultimate ritualistic behavior in chipmunks. If I ever have the opportunity to record one cinematographically, the credits at the end of the film will have to feature "Pageantry by Evolution."

A typical tournament took place on the porch between Fenwick and Kenilworth on February 14, 1976. The location was about forty-five feet from Fenwick's burrow and about 120 feet from Kenilworth's. The latter's willingness to fight that far from home shows the intensity of the aggressive drive during the mating season. The action occurred at a much slower and more deliberate pace than one sees in a typical fight at other times. It is much more ritualistic, shows no indication of murderous intent, and consists primarily of wrestling rather than biting.

The posture of the combatants was stiff-legged, with backs arched. The initial and subsequent Fenwick-Kenilworth encounters began from a side-by-side, head-to-tail, facing position about two feet apart and held for from two to fifteen seconds. One pounced upon the other's back toward the neck, followed by a face-to-face, tummy-to-tummy clinch, a roll, a twist, separation, and refacing. This was repeated six times in two minutes, with Kenilworth initiating contact during the first two trials and Fenwick initiating the last four.

Kenilworth finally fled north—his burrow was to the south—and Fenwick, panting and ruffled, drank from the water dish for almost a minute before he went home

and retired.

The tournament is almost never followed by a chase, and the fact that strength and aggressiveness rather than security are the decisive factors was indicated by Kenilworth's flight away from, rather than toward, home.

On July 10, 1978, Willoughby and Ipswich jousted in the woods at a point equidistant from their individual territories and at the edge of Gutrune's. Willoughby, the elder and more experienced, prevailed over Ipswich, the younger but much larger of the two. The second of only two examples of a chipmunk defeated in its own territory took place under these circumstances.

On February 11, 1976, Diarmuid, a large young chipmunk sixty feet from home, challenged Fenwick about eighteen inches from the latter's burrow entrance. After only four trials, Fenwick escaped into his burrow and Diarmuid remained for several minutes peering into the entrance before going about his business. Fenwick emerged cautiously ten minutes later and remained close to home.

Hannibal's jousting prowess delivered victory after victory and on July 25, 1975, he swept Gutrune off her feet, they mated with a minimal courtship, and he went home to Carthage, not to reappear until the July mating season of the following year. I still wonder where he spent his time during the spring mating seasons.

Gutrune was restored to power and, as a result of this romance, dispersed a litter of three on October 14. One of the three was Guinevere, who settled in a burrow thirty feet northeast of her mother's. Her burrow entrance was in the center of a small circle of crocuses.

Since Guinevere was the first native-born subject, she presented the first opportunity to examine postdispersal parent-offspring interactions. The deference with which Gutrune treated Guinevere is described on page 56, and, although it was observable, it was quite modest. For the remainder of October and November, Guinevere frequently returned to her mother's burrow for the purpose of stealing food when Gutrune was out. On the few occasions on which mother returned home and caught daughter plundering, one would not have thought them to have been related. Gutrune seemed to attack her daughter with all the fury that the situation demanded, but Guinevere always managed to escape without losing her plunder.

Later observations on other family relationships confirmed that this was a typical one. Since a function of aggression is to acquire a greater share of the available resources, parent-offspring aggression after dispersal might not seem to support the concept of kin selection, that is, the directed altruistic behavior toward those who share a major proportion of your genes. However, since food resources are not critical to the survival of the chipmunk, because of the hoarding instinct, these resources can apparently be shared to the needed extent within the aggressive pattern, a pattern that may aim more toward protecting the hoarded provisions.

The first year of the study ended with the usual fall harvest, including Guinevere's harvest from her mother's pantry. Although Gutrune remained active most of the winter, except for three weeks in January, the others retired to hibernation in mid-November. Lady Cheltenham, who had been active the previous winter, retired for eleven weeks on November 22.

In this account of the first year I have presented data from all six years of the study, and the general annual life history of the Eastern chipmunk has been established. Next we turn to the historical aspects of the remaining years and the concept of population dynamics.

7

A Community of the Self-Absorbed

The conclusion of the 1975 season left Gutrune, the unquestioned ruler of the community, entangled in a family squabble with Guinevere, her three-month-old daughter, over pantry rights in the natal burrow. Before discussing population dynamics and the nature of the burrow, a brief summary of the major events that took place during the succeeding seasons, from 1976 through 1980, might be of interest as an aid to filling in the continuity of names mentioned up to this point. The reader is also referred to the biographies of Lady Cheltenham, Gutrune, Mistress Earwicker, and Fenwick in Appendix A and to the legend accompanying figure 11. A history of some of the romances will be found in Appendix E.

The 1976 season found Diarmuid a serious competitor to Fenwick with respect to the ladies. Launcelot, Rinaldo, and Don Diego, along with spring-born Willoughby, formed a minority later in the summer, especially after Diarmuid's disappearance as a result of either death or migration to escape the growing competition. It was at this time that Fenwick moved his quarters in response to Gutrune's imperialistic elaboration of her burrow in the direction of his. When he finally retreated, his entrance was less than ten feet from Gutrune's, and territorial skirmishes occupied a good part of each day.

The summer mating season produced the largest crop of resident juveniles observed during the entire study, including Mistress Earwicker, Mistress Appleford (the mouse hunter), Jellicle, Gustavus Adolphus, and Pumpkinseed. Pumpkinseed, named because he was the only chipmunk who ate what he was named, excavated a simple burrow near the stump separating Gutrune's and Guinevere's territories and failed to reappear from it in the spring.

Gustavus Adolphus, who occupied a burrow beneath a pile of brush, was the only chipmunk active over a winter of severe January ice storms because his entrance was protected while those of the others were plugged tightly with ice. He regularly traveled a distance of almost 120 feet to the porch. His route took him through the territories of several other residents who, when the ground thawed sufficiently to free them from their icy imprisonment, resented Gustavus's trespassing and did something about it. Alas, like his royal patron the Snow King, he fought better on snow than in mud and was unable to continue his foraging so far from home. That icy winter also saw the disappearance of Kenilworth.

The 1977 season saw Launcelot, Willoughby, and Rinaldo completely displace Fenwick's remaining authority, sentencing him to live out his life as a roving adventurer, which he did elegantly. Gutrune's death in July was followed by the systematic looting of her burrow by two of her recently dispersed youngsters, Pilfer and Pillage.

Lady Cheltenham's arthritis reduced her to further withdrawal and she minded her own business. Rinaldo had his last adventures during this summer and Ipswich was the most important juvenile addition during the fall. All of the six-month-old juvenile females from the fall of 1976 mated in the spring and produced families.

During 1978 Ipswich, at six months of age, held his own heroically against the remaining males and became a principal sire. He saw his 1979 challenger, Bohort, born to Guinevere and Willoughby in the fall.

In the 1979 season, in which Fenwick's flaglike tail was seen for the last time answering the mating call, Bohort became a major challenge to Ipswich. This was not a happy year for observation because it witnessed the loss of three principals. Lady Cheltenham's death in March was a major

Figure 62. Don Diego.

Figure 63. Kenilworth.

Figure 64. Willoughby.

Figure 65. Bohort.

Figure 66. Clorindas, the present Squire of Rosyrump.

Figure 67. Winthrop.

disappointment; she had been in burrow no. 1 for over five seasons, since the very beginning of the study. The disappointment was not lessened when Mistress Earwicker, her daughter, was eaten by a pussycat shortly after moving into the ancestral burrow. But the family tradition was carried on when Clorindas, born to Mistress Earwicker and Ipswich during the spring, occupied the family home, and he continues to live there to this day.

The final tragedy was the loss of Jellicle to an automobile on the state road near her burrow. The small pile of stones marking her resting place next to her front door has never been disturbed, and the burrow was promptly occupied by Juliana, her recently dispersed daughter, whose vocal talents still add an air of grace to the neighborhood.

The 1980 season, which began late with no spring mating, saw Ipswich challenged by Winthrop, Wallenstein (he lived in G. Adolphus's burrow), and Clorindas. Bohort failed to reappear. Clorindas became as heroic as his heritage might have suggested. Juliana continued to sing (and warble), and Brunhilde, the battle-scarred, acted as though Gutrune had given her some of her aggressiveness genes.

But by now all of the burrows had changed occupants at least once and all of the oldtimers were gone. As it always seems, the youngsters were and are a mild lot compared with their forebears. The exploits of Fenwick and Lady Cheltenham remain as an epic from a previous age; the songs and trills from the woods always seem to be theirs.

But what of these burrows that had been passed on from one chipmunk to another and form the basis for their sedentary and solitary lives? They are really quite marvelous feats of engineering, and their construction and structure reflect many of the instinctive aspects of the chipmunk's success in the world. They also represent models of efficient land use for the ecological movement, since they involve the removal and rearrangement of great quantities of earth with virtually no alteration of the surface. Chipmunks are not strip miners!

In the sandy gravel of the Fall Line area of Virginia, one can always recognize the entrance to a chipmunk's burrow if one can find it. A circular hole 1½ to two inches in diameter, which extends vertically for at least four inches and shows no evidence of having been dug, is almost invariably the door to a burrow. Usually, burrows are located at the forest edge protected by at least the cover of trees, but may on occasion be found on an open lawn.

The neatness of the entrance discourages discovery by both predators and humans, and the secret of the burrow's neatness was revealed to me one day when Gutrune suddenly appeared from the ground at a location from which she had never appeared previously. As she arose from out of the ground, like Erda the Earth Goddess, a small circular flap of moss was raised by her head like a trap door, and when she left her new entrance, the mossy trap door fell back into place leaving no evidence of the hole. When she returned, it took her about twenty seconds to relocate the entrance, from which she quickly detached the patch of moss, disposing of it in the woods.

Secrecy is protection, of course, but a chipmunk must be able to find its own door quickly in case of emergency and this was carrying secrecy a bit too far. The secret lies in the fact that the entrance is dug from beneath rather than from above the ground, as we shall see from John Burroughs's description later.

Burrows vary in their complexity, but the most elaborate in this study was Lady Cheltenham's (burrow no. 1 in figure 11) with thirty entrances used over her six-season lifetime. Figure 70 shows the positions of the entrances on the surface and the legend describes the order in which they were opened and the pattern in which they were used.

The heading "entrances in use" requires an explanation. Although several entrances may be used during a certain period, only one is open at a time; the others are plugged with earth. I have frequently seen

Figure 68 (top). Lady Cheltenham's burrow entrance no. 3 (ruler graduated in centimeters).

Figure 69. Gutrune's burrow entrance on the lawn (ruler graduated in centimeters).

chipmunks in danger hide in an old burrow entrance, but when the danger had sufficiently abated, they invariably reappeared and dashed swiftly to the current entrance for more permanent safety. This has consistently indicated that old entrances are either temporarily blocked below or no longer connected with the rest of the burrow. Generally, a chipmunk will use only one entrance during a day's activity and all of the others can be demonstrated to be closed. Occasionally, a chipmunk will use one entrance in the morning, retire for a mid-day siesta, and then reappear from a different entrance, but, during a period of activity, it will *always* reenter the one from which it emerged.

The complexity of Lady Cheltenham's entrance pattern shows that the burrow was continuously elaborated, but that toward the end of her career her arthritis may have taken some of the pleasure out of digging. Next to hoarding food, I believe a chipmunk's favorite occupation is digging and, of course, the two are related because it must have places to store the food. We have already seen how sometimes even the current entrance is sealed for the night or during the day if there are children in the burrow.

I can present no observational data on the internal structure of the burrow in this study because I did not want to disturb the peace of the community by digging them out. This is just another way of saying that I did not want to inconvenience my friends, but it is rationalized somewhat by the recognition that digging out a burrow requires the most sophisticated archeological techniques, principally because one encounters no human artifacts that may suggest what is coming next.

Fortunately, for our information rather than the chipmunk's convenience, a number of burrows have been carefully studied and reported in the literature from representative locations within the chipmunk's range. Panuska and Wade uncovered thirty burrows in Wisconsin, Kim R. Thomas excavated fifty in Louisiana,

Lang Elliott studied six in the Adirondack Mountains of New York, and Elsa Allen opened one near Ithaca, New York, Panuska and Wade also studied the structures of burrows built by captive chipmunks in outdoor pens near St. Louis. Most of the observations were quite similar, and they give us confidence in believing that chipmunks dig alike throughout their range.

There is general agreement that chipmunks use two types of burrows. Simple systems consist of one or two tunnels that lead to a single chamber. Their function is not clear, but it has been suggested that simple burrows are only temporary abodes, perhaps used by fall-born chipmunks during their first winter and then either abandoned or elaborated for permanent residence. The one illustrated by Allen in figure 71 is a simple system newly

Figure 70. Map—and log—of Lady Cheltenham's burrow entrances:

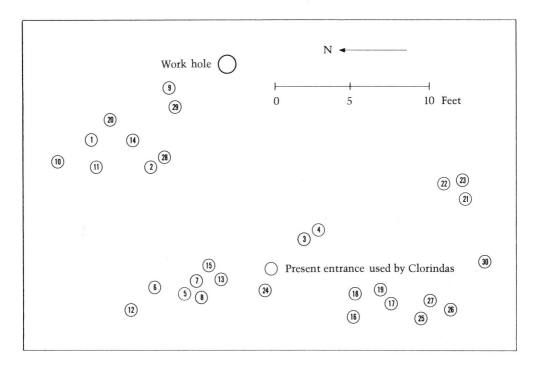

Entrance	Date Opened	Entrances in Use		Entrance	Date Opened	Entrances in Use
1	11/74	1		18	9/22/76	16, 17, 18
2	12/74	2		19	10/5/76	16, 19
3	1/28/75	3				(#16; 10/6–11/26)
4	5/19/75	3, 4		20	12/5/76	20
5	6/2/75	5				(#16; 2/15/77–3/29/77)
6	6/3/75	5, 6		21	3/30/77	21
7	6/6/75	3, 4, 5, 6, 7		22	3/31/77	22
8	6/26/75	3, 4, 6, 7, 8		23	4/2/77	23
9	7/25/75	3, 4, 6, 7, 9		24	4/4/77	13, 14, 15, 24
10	8/14/75	3, 4, 6, 7, 10				(#15; 4/9–5/25)
11	9/1/75	3, 4, 6, 7, 10, 11				(#13; 5/26–6/9)
		(#3; 9/22–11/22)				(#15; 10/11–11/9)
12	2/18/76	7, 8, 12		25	3/12/78	25
13	4/4/76	7, 8, 10, 13		26	4/19/78	26
14	6/14/76	13, 14		27	5/17/78	27
15	6/21/76	13, 15		28	8/19/78	28
16	8/27/76	16		29	8/23/78	28, 29
17	8/30/76	16, 17		30	2/28/79	30

Figure 71. Diagram of a newly constructed simple burrow (after Allen, 1938). Courtesy of New York State Museum.

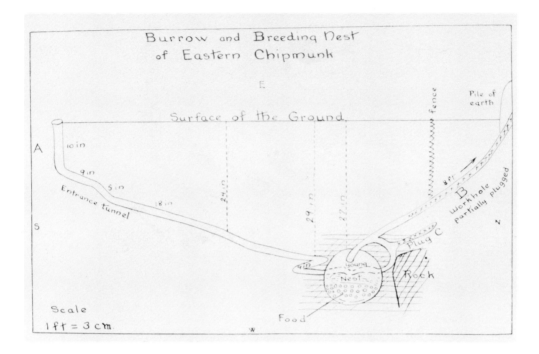

excavated by a young female close to a prosperous feeding site and was probably destined to become more complex. Thomas has suggested that simple burrows may be used as invertebrate traps, that is, they may serve as a place in which chipmunks can always find animal goodies for their diet. In the present study, the small number of entrances close together used by many of the males may indicate that, since they do not raise families, some males may continue to live in modestly simple burrow systems.

Extensive burrow systems, like Lady Cheltenham's, are far more complex, containing many tunnels and chambers. The literature indicates that they may have up to five entrances, this being the maximum number observed among the more than eighty burrows studied. By these standards, Lady Cheltenham's, with thirty entrances, is a palace and, were Clorindas not happily in occupancy, I would be overcome by curiosity to see if it has central heating and oriental carpets.

Extensive systems described in the literature have up to one hundred feet of tunnels, twenty-five-by-fifteen-by-ten-inch nesting chamber, an average of three additional ten-by-fifteen-by-six-inch storage chambers, and up to eight smaller rooms. In addition, the *pro tem* archeologists encountered numerous side pockets, sometimes referred to as blind tunnels or galleries. All dimensions given here are averages and are, therefore, approximate. Most of the chambers have at least two entrances, and the tunnels connecting them are three to four inches in diameter. Thomas encountered a bypass tunnel where a single one diverged into two, one above the other, rejoined after about ten inches. This was speculated to serve either as a traffic control point when young lived in the burrow or as a means of allowing the occupant to double back when escaping

Colorplate 16. The escape leap: acrobatics of survival. Lady Cheltenham was feeding peacefully when she was attacked by a less than gallant Don Diego. She executed this escape leap, followed by a somersault to the ground, and avoided another fight. Unexplained, this photograph could be interpreted quite differently.

Colorplate 17. The roll-tumble fight: Lady Cheltenham and Fenwick mix it up. This is what results when both parties stand their ground. The weaker of the two will kick free shortly and retreat.

pursuit by a predator. Both tunnels and chambers were observed with tree-root pillars and with rocks and roots forming the sides and roof, but not the floor. This suggests that when a chipmunk reaches an obstruction that cannot be removed, it burrows either to one side or below it rather than running the risk of returning to the surface by burrowing above it.

The depth of the burrows was five to seventeen inches in warm Louisiana and twenty-five to thirty inches in cold Wisconsin. In both areas, the burrows do not penetrate the frost line. In some cases, the nesting chamber, the largest of the compartments, contained the remains of a fifteen-by-eight-inch nest formed from dry leaves that appeared to have been chewed into half-inch pieces for better insulation. The nests, however, did not fill the chambers. The cleanliness of the chipmunk has been confirmed by the universal absence of feces in the burrow. Anecdotal tales of toilet chambers have not been confirmed.

Food stored in the auxiliary chambers amounted to little in Wisconsin, moderate quantities in Louisiana, and large quantities in New York. The capacity for storage was discussed in chapter 2 with reference to the observations of Burroughs and Elliott. Segregated storerooms for different types of food have been observed, but rather than suggesting the kind of orderly stewardship indicated by the chipmunk's generic name, *Tamias*, segregation of acorns into one chamber, seeds into another, etc., probably reflects the fact that each of these stores was collected during a discrete period of time when the seasonal food was available, and it was simply placed in the storeroom being filled at the time.

In summary, the burrow can be seen to be a remarkable feat of construction, but the manner in which it is constructed is even more remarkable. Only one man, to my knowledge, has actually seen and described a burrow excavated. John Burroughs observed a young chipmunk at work in his apple orchard. Although occasionally his conclusions have been questioned, even by

himself, I am not aware of any criticism of the accuracy of his observations.

Burroughs described his chipmunk as "... using his nose as a shovel ... digging and pushing the soil up to the mouth of his hole, and then pushing it ... to the dump heap." He went on to say how "... at the final stroke, the soil, a half-teaspoonful or more, would shoot from his nose four or five inches." Such was the energy of his activity, we gather from this description, that the chipmunk must have delighted in it and "... as he turned back ... he would rapidly paw the earth behind him.... As he entered his hole, a succession of quick jets of earth, forming little parabolas in the air, would shoot up behind him." For nearly three weeks the chipmunk worked at his new home with "... every motion repeated like clockwork." During this time a "plump bushel" of soil was brought to the surface.

Apparently the earth is dug by biting and scratching motions and moved with the nose in bulldozer fashion. The presence of pellets of earth on a dump pile led Elsa Allen to conclude that the soil was sometimes carried in the cheek pouches. There is none but the most circumstantial evidence for this and it appears to have never been observed directly. Certainly Burroughs's chipmunk did not do it, for he stated in his already quoted account that "I used to think that the chipmunk carried away the soil in his cheek pouches, and have so-stated in one of my books [*Riverby*, 1894], but I am now certain that he does not—only his food stores are thus carried."

He went on to ask why the chipmunk has not evolved a shovellike nose. One answer to this question would seem to be that the selective pressure has not been great enough since many, or even most, chipmunks move into previously occupied burrows and probably very few are forced to construct an entire system in a short period of time. The continuous work done in elaboration of the burrow is not accomplished under the same pressure.

The terrible mess made by his little friend suggested to Burroughs that he was

Figure 72. Gutrune's work hole (ruler graduated in centimeters).

Figure 73. Ipswich's burrow entrance in the snow.

inexperienced, but his strategy became clear after about three weeks when he began closing the entrance: "while I was looking, the closure was completed from within." During the next day or two, the chipmunk covered this closed work hole with the soil from the dump pile and opened, from below, two new clean entrances nearby.

The ingenious process can best be seen with reference to figure 71. Imagine the chipmunk beginning at the upper right of the figure and digging down while moving the earth out through the work hole to form the pile pictured. The process continues until the nest chamber at the center has been constructed and the entrance tunnel to the left has been almost completed back to the surface. It might seem wasteful for the chipmunk to move soil from the upper portions of the entrance tunnel all the way back, through the nest chamber, and out the work hole, but the result is worth the effort. When the working tunnel on the right has been filled in with the soil from the last few inches of the entrance tunnel on the left, the chipmunk has a clean entrance hole opened from below, remote from any evidence of digging and, therefore, safe from easy location by predators.

This strategy reminds us of Franz Kafka's unnamed animal in his short story "The Burrow." The animal takes justly great pride and care in the security of its burrow, but the story is too anthropomorphic to be taken seriously and the outcome is unpleasantly reminiscent of Kafka's view of the world.

Figure 72 shows a work hole used by Gutrune for the enlargement of her burrow in the spring of 1975, the process that eventually led to Fenwick's relocation. The hole was almost four inches in diameter, and the size of some of the rocks that she removed is a tribute to her bulldozerlike personality. The work hole was located about fifteen feet from her active entrance and the dirt pile, although small, remained for some time as an unsightly mess on the lawn.

There can be no doubt that a chipmunk's subterranean castle is constructed with the advantages of a long history of adaptive wisdom. Incidentally, the best time to locate chipmunk burrows is in the early spring after an unseasonal snow storm. Figure 73 illustrates Ipswich's entrance in March 1978.

The understanding of the sophisticated nature of the Eastern chipmunk's burrow

Colorplates 18 and 19. Battle scars—the badges of courage. Although severe wounds seldom result from fighting, Brunhilde (top) wears the scar and torn left ear of a heroic encounter. Gutrune (bottom) exhibits the coat of many battles, none of them severe. In a few weeks she will molt and acquire a new and perfect coat. Brunhilde has already molted and will wear her badge throughout her life.

leads, in turn, to an understanding of the animal's sedentary nature and solitary behavior. It is not difficult to see why chipmunks, after all the work that went into preparing and provisioning the home, are willing and anxious to protect their investment aggressively. The result is territoriality, which has a significant influence on population density. The level of population, or its density, reflects the three things that an animal requires—food, space, mates—for success in the world. These three requirements conform with Lorenz's great parliament of instincts. Hunger is satisfied with food; love is satisfied with mates; flight and fight are regulated by space. Love establishes the minimum density.

Extremely sparse populations might seem to be ideal because food would always be plentiful and aggressive encounters would be so infrequent that energy would not be wasted in fighting and there would little danger of injury. On the other hand, the lower limit is set by the possibility under these circumstances that the low encounter rate would not permit estrous females to find willing males at the proper time. The population could then decline to extinction. This does not occur because, like most organisms, the chipmunk overproduces young. A single female may produce eight or ten per year and heaven only knows how many an active male may sire. The maximum population density is, therefore, of more concern. Factors limiting population size are weather, food supply, and predators.

The population figures for the 1½-acre area of this study are presented in figure 74. These figures have the disadvantage of representing a small area, but they have the advantage of being accurate. They represent, in the case of those labeled residents, the actual identification of who was living in which of the thirty burrows during each season. They show the average population throughout the season, ignoring the fact that, for example, five adults (three females and two males) and fifteen juveniles occupied an area of 0.1 acre during part of May 1976, just prior to dispersal. Trapping studies carried out during this short period would obviously have presented an entirely different picture.

The population densities, which are based on the residents only, are actually quite constant over the six-year period for a locality as small and as carefully defined as this one. I would tend to conclude that the population is well represented by the average figure of 12.9 per acre. The sex ratios varied between 30 and 60 percent males and 40 to 70 percent females for an average of 40 percent males and 60 percent females as compared with Yerger's average figures of 45 and 55 percent. Again, the variation seems to be consistent with the small area studied.

Winter survival figures are not presented

Figure 74. The local chipmunk population over a six-year period.

	1975	1976	1977	1978	1979	1980
Resident males	7	9	10	5	4	6
Resident females	7	6	12	11	9	12
Resident juveniles	3	8	4	1	2	0
Transient males	1	3	1	3	4	3
Transient females	4	5	4	4	4	1
Transient juveniles	1	0	7	7	1	0
Density (per acre)	11.3	15.3	17.3	11.3	10.0	12.0

because the ease of migration makes it impossible to distinguish death and emigration. This is a problem with any population study no matter how large the area, although the larger the area, the less significant it becomes. One interesting feature of figure 74 is the above-average population density in 1977, which must have resulted partly from the large number of resident juveniles incorporated during 1976. There was a continual migration into the area as those chipmunks living in less desirable ranges moved into better burrows here as they became available.

Even within the area there was a continual shifting of burrows as youngsters in marginal or temporary burrows moved into the more desirable ones. Gutrune's arrival in 1975 and the occupation of the ancestral home of Lady Cheltenham by her daughter and grandson are but two examples. The legend accompanying figure 11 is a record of all such migrations.

The only large-scale systematic study of chipmunk populations was that of C. A. Tryon and D. P. Snyder on two sites in western Pennsylvania from 1962 to 1970 and on one site in southern Vermont from 1965 to 1970. The areas of these sites were approximately 7.5, 6.7, and 22 acres respectively. The study method was systematic trapping, identification, and release. No burrows were located and a resident was defined as a chipmunk identified during two or more successive years. The question of emigration vs. mortality was minimized by the sizes of the sites, but was still recognized. An impressive record of 50,112 captures of 4,000 chipmunks, 1,580 of which were first captured as juveniles, provides sufficient data to establish the detailed life tables presented. A summary of some of these data is rearranged in figure 75.

A maximum observed age of twelve to thirteen years, and an average lifespan of 1.29 years, make the Eastern chipmunk a relatively long-lived rodent when compared with one year for the gray squirrel and 0.25 to 0.75 year for smaller rodents. The average population densities were approxi-

Figure 75. Life expectancy for chipmunks of known age (rearranged from Tryon and Snyder, 1973).

Age	Pennsylvania – 1				Pennsylvania – 2				Vermont			
	Spring		Fall		Spring		Fall		Spring		Fall	
	Male	Female	Male	Female	Male	Female	Male	Female	Male	Female	Male	Female
0– 1	3.05	2.36	2.09	2.36	4.53	3.35	2.06	1.94	2.12	2.66	1.86	2.60
1– 2	3.36	2.45	2.56	3.63	6.11	3.40	4.53	4.30	1.45	2.01	2.66	2.78
2– 3	3.52	2.82	2.17	3.91	5.95	3.83	4.13	4.06	1.58	2.60	2.50	2.15
3– 4	3.14	2.94	2.29	3.86	6.38	3.38	2.66	5.06	1.08	2.01	2.32	2.64
4– 5	3.62	2.89	1.89	4.75	8.65	3.28	2.69	5.12	1.38	2.29	1.72	2.60
5– 6	3.21	2.81	2.62	4.36	7.65	2.68	2.21	6.17	0.90	1.39	2.64	1.83
6– 7	2.67	2.83	1.93	3.65	5.01	2.89	1.21	5.17	1.50	1.50	2.50	1.00
7– 8	2.10	2.13	2.83	3.23	4.01	2.57	1.50	5.50	0.50	0.50	1.50	1.50
8– 9	1.90	1.67	1.83	2.50	2.65	5.30	0.50	4.50			0.50	0.50
9–10	1.25	1.83	1.50	1.04	1.65	4.30		3.50				
10–11	0.50	1.50	0.50	0.50	1.55	2.67		2.50				
11–12		0.50			1.59	1.67		1.50				
12–13					1.50	0.50		0.50				
13–14					0.50							

mately thirty and twenty-five per acre on the Pennsylvania sites and ten per acre on the Vermont location. Figure 75 shows the average number of years a chipmunk reaching a particular age may be expected to live beyond that age. These are the same kinds of statistics upon which our life insurance premiums are based and it is both comforting and discomforting to know that insurance companies do not seem to lose money. The table shows clearly that the first year is critical. During the subsequent years life expectancy increases until old age takes over somewhere between five and eight years. The average lifespan of 1.29 years results from very high juvenile mortality.

It can also be seen that spring-born chipmunks survive better than fall-born ones. This makes sense since the spring-born animal has more time to become established before the rigors of winter set in. The disparity is not as great as it might seem that it should be, however, probably because fall-born chipmunks know where the acorns are when they are dispersed, whereas spring-born chipmunks must establish a home without this knowledge. The authors suggest the possibility of a three- or four-year synchronized population cycle at all three locations. The limited data in the present study might seem to suggest the same thing, but Lawrence B. Slobodkin has repeatedly warned that the manipulation of data frequently produces only a superficial appearance of population cycles.

The factors that must be considered in limiting overpopulation of chipmunks fall into three convenient categories: food supply, territoriality, and predation. The chipmunk's hoarding instinct might seem to eliminate food supply from the list since chipmunks hoard much more food than they need, but the absence of food to gather affects their well-being by denying them an instinctively given right. It is possible that hibernation is initiated partially out of boredom when the fall harvest is exhausted and Elsa Allen has reported that, in winter,

active chipmunks survive better than those in hibernation.

Since chipmunks acquire their hoards by scramble foraging, as opposed to contest foraging, survival during the first season may depend upon the availability of food. The newly dispersed juvenile must find and stock a burrow before winter and must compete, in this respect, with its more experienced elders. A plentiful acorn crop will aid materially in that critical first-season survival. After the burrow is established and initially stocked, food supply probably has little effect on future survival and, therefore, on further population regulation, since chipmunks are not disposed to abandon a well-provided home.

Territoriality defines the maximum population density, because every chipmunk requires at least a minimum amount of elbow room and there must be a point beyond which this space cannot be further compressed by population growth. A growing population produces an increase in the encounter rate between chipmunks. The result is both obvious and subtle. An abnormally high encounter rate leads to frequent fighting, which robs the chipmunk of time and energy for more useful pursuits like mating, food hoarding, and digging. It also leads to many alterations in the endocrine or hormonal system of physiological regulation.

It has been shown in other animal populations that dominance status determines the blood levels of androgenic hormones secreted by the adrenal cortex and subordinate animals show higher levels of pituitary-adrenal activity. John J. Christian has proposed a theory of population stabilization based upon this phenomenon. In summary, it states that high aggressive encounter rates lead to enlarged adrenal glands, which may result in kidney failure, impaired antibody formation and increased susceptibility to disease, lowered fertility, and even death.

I. L. Ward observed an even more subtle phenomenon in rats. Pregnant females exposed to stress showed higher androgen levels and produced male offspring that demonstrated degrees of bisexual behavior. Their behavior appeared to be demasculinized in their relations with females and feminized in their relations with other males. Since sex is not fully determined until the later stages of development, Ward suggests that the high androgen levels in the mother may inhibit the complete defeminization of the brains of the developing males. These bisexually oriented males would then breed less efficiently and the result would be a smaller next generation.

F. V. Clulow and colleagues tested aspects of Christian's theory by confining dense populations of chipmunks on lake islands in Canada. The densities varied between twenty and 150 per acre initially and between ten and thirty per acre after the populations had stabilized. Approximately 40 percent of the chipmunks were recovered and their adrenal glands were examined. The results showed a definite correlation between population density and adrenal activity in chipmunks. Curiously, the same result was not observed with white-footed mice. These physiological phenomena, then, must tend to limit population expansion beyond a certain point. Although chipmunks are sedentary animals, this sedentary behavior is not evident until the latter part of the first season when they have established a burrow, and until that time, the active dispersal we examined in chapter 4 serves to allow the population density to stabilize.

Chipmunk populations are remarkably stable. There is, to my knowledge, no record of a catastrophic chipmunk explosion anywhere. It does not seem to be necessary for them to march, like lemmings, into the sea periodically or to require, like gray squirrels, park service personnel to physically remove portions of an overly suburbanized community.

How much predators contribute is difficult to estimate. Chipmunk predators in this area include domestic cats, hawks, and large snakes. Because they are the most common, domestic cats are probably the most significant, although I have only infrequently seen them successful. I have seen the others try but not succeed. In other areas, weasels and rats are reported to be the most dangerous, because they are small enough to pursue a chipmunk into the burrow. Audubon and John Bachman have described the weasel's terrible work and I will leave the gruesome details to them.

Population density of a prey species is always proportional to predator interest in that species as long as the predator population is normal. Predators are good at removing the weaker animals, but turn their interest elsewhere when the particular prey species becomes scarce. This is a smart move. They do not eat themselves into extinction. Of course, predators have their own population problems and we saw in this area an increase in the hawk population during 1976. The numbers of hawks sighted and the numbers of attacks observed were at their highest levels then than at any other time during the six years of the study. They did not, however, seem to be any more successful than at other times and by 1977 the normal population level appeared to have been restored. The increase of hawks in 1976 may have been in response to an abundance of mice or some other species. Chipmunks may have been considered dessert.

Many suburban dwellers have observed chipmunks on their property in some years and not in others. In every case of this sort that I have investigated, the disappearance and appearance have been correlated with the immigration and emigration of neighbors with dogs and cats; in other words, with the population of specific predators. Chipmunks will not tolerate ignorant predators. Domestic dogs and cats do not hunt in order to eat and, therefore, do not stop when their hunger is satisfied.

Chipmunks are so fastidious about their habitat and sensitive to the intensity of predation that predators cannot rely on them exclusively. If a local population is

Colorplate 20. Spiritual sustenance? Diarmuid dines with the cardinal. This scene is not as peaceful as it seems. The camera's ability to freeze 1/3000 second in time necessitates knowledge of the context of the photograph in order for the viewer to interpret the action. The cardinal was feeding on the log, and the picture was taken just as Diarmuid, with a sunflower seed in his mouth, appeared. Within a fraction of a second both had fled the scene. Note that, even at this stage of the action, Diarmuid's ears are back in an aggressive response. The cardinal has not yet realized that he has company.

demolished, it will spring up again as a result of dispersal from a nearby range as soon as the predator population returns to normal or the source of predation is removed.

In this chapter we have seen many examples of the wisdom of nature that manifests itself in such a way as to appear to be the wisdom of the chipmunk. Chipmunks are, indeed, wise creatures, but only because natural selection is the wisdom of nature.

Having now completed our study of what chipmunks do, and leaving our area under the firm control of Clorindas, the Squire of Rosyrump, and with the gracious song of Juliana, the siren, we turn in the next chapter to a brief consideration of why chipmunks do what they do.

8

The Evolution of Independence

No one can say when the appropriate genes appeared that led the first solitary chipmunk on its road to independence, but that those genes have been serviceable is obvious. They have met the test of natural selection for 25 million years while many other squirrels and mammals have moved toward socialization. A chipmunk with social tendencies appearing in a present-day population is sure to get clobbered.

In the first seven chapters, I have often spoken of the selective value, the adaptive value, or the fitness of a particular behavior or characteristic, but the observation of these sometimes obvious features does not mean that they have actually been selected during the course of evolution. Nonetheless, the Eastern chipmunk today represents the final results of a succession of evolutionary changes that have been successful. The adaptiveness of structure and behavior is one of the most popular speculative biological procedures today. It reasons that a physical or behavioral characteristic is adaptive if it promotes an individual's opportunity for survival or reproductive success. But, as Luigi L. Cavalli-Sforza and Marucs Feldman have pointed out, we must not expect to observe any but the most obvious adaptations to the most common and dramatic challenges by the environment.

The ability of living things to endure environmental changes has been so successful that it may lead us into teleological reasoning; the search for a profound adaptive significance of every observed behavior or physical characteristic, no matter how trivial. The adaptiveness, especially, of behavior is often far from obvious, and may not even exist. In any case, proving it poses monumental difficulties.

Fitness is, of course, Darwinian fitness, the same thing as the adaptiveness of a biological trait measured in terms of the number of off-spring that survive to matur-

ity produced by the individuals possessing the trait. The more fit the animal, the greater its capacity to leave progeny. Fitness has been estimated in two ways: by using Ronald A. Fisher's classical formula based on age-specific birth and death rates and by measuring actual changes in the gene frequencies of a population over a period of time. In the second case, the time period must cover a number of generations; therefore, it is not a quick process. There also must exist the possibility of comparing members of the same population that possess and that lack the specific characteristic.

One of the signatures of the chipmunk is its alertness behavior, its characteristic ability to interrupt the most absorbing tasks every few seconds in order to determine what may be sneaking up on it. Is this behavior adaptive in terms of a chipmunk's survival? Surely it must be, but with what can we compare it? I have never observed a chipmunk lacking this behavior, possibly because one lacking it would not be around long enough to be observed. Such behaviors are called innate because they are inborn and, therefore, genetically determined.

Let us now examine some of the chipmunk's previously described characteristic behaviors that may be adaptive and see if we can come to some conclusion regarding the certainty, or lack thereof, of their adaptiveness. There is indirect evidence for the adaptiveness of the chipmunk's obsessional food hoarding as a winter survival substitute for hibernation. Brenner and Lyle have suggested that food-hoarding behavior has been selected in this way. It has been shown that winter survival is greater among active chipmunks than those in hibernation. The food stores allow hibernation to be avoided or at least modified to comprise only short periods of torpidity. Furthermore, the safety of the hoard from

Colorplate 21. Lady Cheltenham poses for the naturalist. This typical and informative pose should be referred to for descriptive purposes while reading Chapter 9 and Appendix D.

Figure 76. *"What's all this about evolution!
I've been here all along."*

Figure 77. *Is sulking adaptive!*

spoilage is strengthened by the chipmunk's innate ability to discriminate between perishable and nonperishable foods.

The independence of the adult chipmunk from the local food supply, except in the sense of depriving it of carrying out its instinctive harvesting program, certainly seems adaptive, especially in time of famine. On the other hand, we cannot be certain that chipmunks are not evolving toward hibernation rather than away from it. It just seems reasonable that food hoarding and hibernation are related and that the former is the more significant.

The nature of the chipmunk's burrow, the seat of its sedentary existence, is beautifully complex, and its manner of construction shows behavior that even seems intelligent by human standards. The effort exerted toward concealment from predators, to the extreme of the animal's apparently innate reticence to disclose the entrance to anyone it knows is watching, as well as such details as always digging around or below obstructions, seem to be quite logically adaptive.

Within the context of mating behavior,

the ritualistic male tournaments and the chase tactics resorted to by females would seem to fall into the same category. The whole nature of the chipmunk's territoriality, within but not throughout the home range, and its ritualized aggressive behavior for the presumed purpose of avoiding energy waste and injury are more examples that, along with the epideictic vocalization during dispersal, literally cry out to be labeled adaptive. However, since we cannot find a chipmunk that does not exhibit these behaviors, we have no basis for assessing their selective value at all quantitatively and we can only guess that they have contributed to the evolution of the chipmunks we know today. We have no evidence for what, if any, selective process is going on at the present time.

The Eastern chipmunk seems to have changed very little since the Miocene, 25 million years ago. Put another way, we can say that, within the particular habitat that it likes best, the chipmunk has not speciated and, therefore, its adaptation to that environment is at least satisfactory, at best nearly perfect. If, as Craig Black has sug-

Figure 78. The nobility of character and elegance of independence: Pickwick looks at the world over his shoulder.

gested, the other members of the squirrel family have evolved from an ancestral chipmunk, this is further evidence of its fitness. It shows the chipmunk's ability to adapt genetically to the Oligocene and Miocene changes described in chapter 1, and, as Lawrence Slobodkin and Anatol Rapoport have pointed out, a population that has descendants, even if these are called by a different species name, is evolutionarily successful, for it has effectively placed its genes in the succeeding generations.

The chipmunk itself has not become extinct following the speciation among its individuals because it is so well adapted to the habitat in which it continues to exist and, to quote these same authors: "At the extreme, we may expect that organisms which have met all the vagaries of their environment by tactical adjustments that do not involve genetic change will never speciate." What are and have been these tactical adjustments? Or, to follow the game theory proposed by Slobodkin and Rapoport, how does the chipmunk minimize its stakes in the game of "Gambler's Ruin" with the outcome of either survival or extinction?

Since its existence is sedentary, confined to a small home range, the chipmunk is likely to experience dramatic environmental changes during each generation and these challenges must be met behaviorally since they cannot, within a generation, be met genetically. The sum and common denominator of the presumably adaptive behaviors discussed above is unquestionably the versatility that arises from independence and solitary existence. Call it enterprise, opportunism, or what you will, this most characteristic feature of the Eastern chipmunk results in the ultimate adaptability to environmental changes. Man's intrusion into the chipmunk's environment has been taken advantage of admirably. While other species have suffered at our hands, the chipmunk has utilized the increased area of forest edge, its favorite habitat, resulting from land development through the dispersal of its young into these new, often suburban, areas. Enterprise and opportunism have allowed the chipmunk to avail itself of all of the benefits. while independence has allowed it to remain undomesticated. From the Eastern chipmunk we have learned the lesson of how an animal survives and prospers by minding its own business.

9

Summary of the Life History of the Eastern Chipmunk

Appearance

The Eastern chipmunk, *Tamias striatus*, is a small diurnal squirrel whose appearance identifies it unmistakably in the eastern half of North America. Represented by only a single species, it is easily distinguished from the several species of Western chipmunk by the characteristically striped pattern of its coat. The underparts are white or light tan with grayish brown above and including nine stripes along the back beginning at the head and shoulders and ending at the typically reddish rump. The head displays two additional dark longitudinal stripes, one through the eye and the other beneath. These facial stripes identify chipmunks the world over (see colorplate 21, page 110).

Typical adult size is between two and three ounces in weight, head and body length of five to six inches, and tail length of three to four inches. By contrast, the western species all have longer tails. The tail is fully furred but not bushy. The chipmunk has a scampering-type skeleton and its external appearance is intermediate between fossorial (burrowing) and arboreal (tree living) shapes. Five functional toes on the hind foot, four on the front foot, eight mammae, and a set of internal cheek pouches complete the picture. Internally, its skull structure establishes its identity to systematists and its dental pattern consists of twenty teeth arranged with one set of incisors, one set of premolars, and three sets of molars in each jaw. Its western cousins have an additional set of premolars in the upper jaw. A detailed description appears in Appendix D.

Appearance remains constant throughout life. There is no external difference in appearance between the sexes except the obvious anatomical characteristics of the genitalia during periods of fertility. Molt occurs once or twice annually, during May or June and sometimes again in October. Although the chipmunk stands out to us in its environment once we have learned to look for it, it actually blends in rather well and is probably quite efficiently camouflaged from the poorly understood vision of its predators. Both albino and melano specimens have been observed, but without geographical regularity. Other identifying features include the characteristic postures illustrated throughout this book.

Classification and Origin

First described in Mark Catesby's *The Natural History of Carolina* (1743), named *Sciurus striatus* from the Greek for striped scourer in 1758 by Linnaeus, and finally reclassified as *Tamias striatus* (striped steward) by Johann Illiger in 1811, the Eastern chipmunk remains somewhat controversial in its relationship with the western and asiatic species. Arthur H. Howell (1929), supported by John A. White (1953), assigned the genus *Tamias*, with twenty teeth, to the Eastern chipmunk, and the genus *Eutamias*, with twenty-two teeth, to all others, allowing the subgenera *Eutamias* for the asiatic and *Neotamias* for the western American natives. J. R. Ellerman (1940) assigned the genus *Tamias* to all chipmunks, no matter how many teeth, allowing three subgenera, *Tamias, Eutamias*, and *Neotamias*, according to the geographic ranges. Various recent studies, mostly involving analysis of the chipmunk's thirty-eight chromosomes, have seemed at times to support both classifications. American mammalogists generally follow Howell, but many Europeans do not, so the literature must be interpreted carefully.

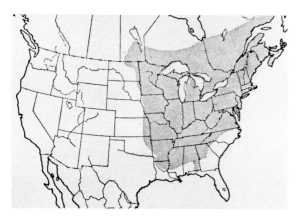

Figure 79. The range of the Eastern chipmunk.

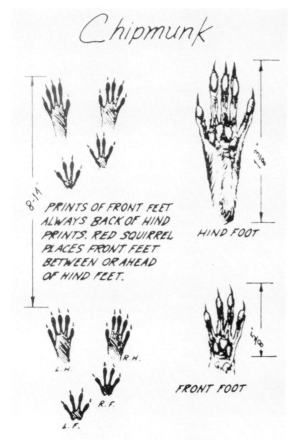

Chipmunk

PRINTS OF FRONT FEET ALWAYS BACK OF HIND PRINTS. RED SQUIRREL PLACES FRONT FEET BETWEEN OR AHEAD OF HIND FEET.

HIND FOOT

FRONT FOOT

Figure 80. Chipmunk tracks. Courtesy Virginia Commission on Game and Inland Fisheries.

The origin of the name chipmunk is not clear, but is usually assumed to come from the American Indian "Adjidaumo," pronounced a-chit-ä-mauk, through the intermediary form of chitmunk. The Indian term refers to red squirrels and means "head-first," describing the manner in which squirrels descend trees, rather than "tail-in-air" as translated by Longfellow in the "song of Hiawatha." The first accurate illustration of the chipmunk appeared in Audubon and Bachman's *Quadrupeds of North America* in 1846.

The fossil record shows the genus *Tamias* as being one of the oldest genera of living squirrels, essentially unchanged since the Miocene epoch almost 25 million years ago. Craig Black, who visualized "the ancestral squirrels as being chipmunk-like," proposed a phylogeny in 1963 in which *Tamias* appeared on the trunk. The newer squirrels seemed to have evolved during the Miocene, when the Great Plains gradually changed from forest to grassland. The chipmunk, with the versatility of its underground home and the ability to range on the surface and into the trees, could have been selected to sponsor tree-living and burrowing descendants and to maintain its own versatility up to the present time. It is this versatility of existence that is responsible for its characteristic independence.

More recent information has, however, produced the family tree shown in figure 3 in which the recent squirrels, including the chipmunks, arise from an arboreal lineage. This new concept only modestly alters the venerability of the chipmunk's existence and does not alter its staying power in the game of evolution.

Range and Habitat

Although the fossil record indicates that the range of *Tamias* probably included most of North America at one time, the Eastern chipmunk is now concentrated in the eastern part of the continent. General boundaries include the Fall Line in the east and south, the timbered regions of Canada in the north, and just beyond the Mississippi in the west. The overall range is inhabited by twelve subspecies distinguishable by slight color and size differences.

Within this range, the Eastern chipmunk is almost invariably found in its favorite habitat, which is upland forest edge of either oak-hickory or maple-beech persuasion. It prefers the forest edge because of its access to the cover and nutty bounty provided by the trees as well as the seeds and fruits of the neighboring open land, and for these reasons it is frequently found in areas bordering towns and subdivisions where man has extended the desirability of habitat by invading the forest and thereby lengthening the forest edge.

Because, to some degree, of the variability of its habitat, the chipmunk's home range is also quite seasonably variable and must be observed throughout the animal's full year of harvesting and mating activities. The most accurate home-range measurements appear to be about 0.5 acre for females, 1.0 acre for males, and 0.2 acre for juveniles of both sexes. The actual range shifts as different fruits, nuts, and seeds ripen, and as the population density changes. The home range of one chipmunk also may overlap the home ranges of others.

The home range of the chipmunk is considered to be relatively permanent. Juveniles may travel great distances before settling, but once settled, adult females almost never relocate and adult males move only very short distances in response to their romantic tendencies.

In their travels, both within and outside their home ranges, chipmunks utilize a scampering bound of about eight to twenty inches, during which the forefeet are placed behind the hind feet. They tend to travel regular routes between landmarks, since their eyes are only an inch or so from the ground and shortened visibility requires navigation based upon taller objects. They climb as adeptly as tree squirrels but, unlike their arboreal relatives, do not jump from branch to branch. Also unlike their

arboreal relatives, they do not fall out of trees. On rare occasions, chipmunks have been observed swimming in still water at rates of about seven miles per hour. Anecdotal reports indicate that chipmunks may be able to find their way back home when displaced from distances of up to 300 or 500 feet.

Private Life—Daily Behavior

Chipmunks are active between dawn and dusk and, therefore, have little to fear from night predators unless these predators are capable of entering the burrow. Their activity is influenced very little by the weather. They can be seen enjoying torrential rain or even a jaunt across the snow if the surface is frozen. I have, on rare occasions, seen them active at temperatures as low as minus 2°F, although they were usually sunning themselves in protected locations, and as high as 104°F, when they usually prefer the cooler climate of the burrow and remain inside while the sun is at its highest angle. The question of estivation, or summer inactivity, has not been resolved, but in this area chipmunks remain active, although they are seen less often because of the density of plant growth and the closeness of food to their burrows. Two factors that encourage inactivity are wind, especially with blowing leaves, and exceptionally dry weather. The former is probably a psychological influence, for chipmunks are easily startled, and the latter is probably because of the close proximity of their noses to the dusty ground.

Cleanliness. As with many animal species, grooming is not only performed for the sake of cleanliness, but also as a displacement activity out of nervous self-consciousness in social situations. Consequently, a self-respecting chipmunk is seldom seen with a hair out of place. They are able to reach all parts of their bodies with either the mouth or the paws. They frequently wash behind their ears by first licking their wrists and paws. Special attention is given to the tail by whisking through the mouth and over the tongue, a procedure facilitated by the space between the incisors and the single set of premolars. As a result of their obsessive cleanliness, they have few external parasites. Although observed generally and frequently in cooler climates, the Cuterebra (Bot) seems to be rare in Virginia chipmunks. It only appeared in one of the six years of this study. They are said to carry the La Cross virus in Ohio and Wisconsin and spotted fever in Canada, but there is no evidence of their ever having transmitted either to humans.

Food and Water. Chipmunks appear to require very little water. I have observed females in lactation remaining in the burrow for several days at a time. In the laboratory, Panuska and Wade have reported that chipmunks drink about one ounce per day when fed dry rations. They drink by slurping rather than lapping.

Food preferences, described in detail in chapter 2, include mainly nuts, seeds, and berries, with a small supplement of animal protein, especially for pregnant and lactating females and for juveniles. Much of a chipmunk's active life is spent searching for food and carrying it home in its capacious cheek pouches. Such tremendous quantities of nonperishable food are stored in the burrow that it is difficult to believe an adult chipmunk ever went hungry. This year-round harvest is responsible for the seasonal shifts in home range.

Burrow and Nesting. The entrance to a chipmunk burrow is a circular hole about two inches in diameter, which descends vertically for at least four inches before sloping off at about a 45-degree angle. The entrance may be found virtually anywhere within the home range and is characterized most significantly by the fact that it is perfectly clean, that is, there is no trace of its having been excavated. While males sometimes live in simple burrows, the most complex structure I have observed was

excavated by a female who used thirty different entrances over a period of six seasons. While a particular entrance was in use, all of the others were closed off from below. The burrow usually consists of an entrance tunnel leading to one or more nesting and storage chambers slightly less than a yard below the surface. The chambers are usually oblong, about the size of a football, and the connecting tunnels may extend over a distance of thirty feet. Construction is carried out through a "working tunnel," out of which all of the dirt and rocks are removed by use of the nose and feet. The entrance tunnel is excavated last, from beneath, and the dirt taken from it is used to fill in the working tunnel. Because the burrow is opened from below, there is no sign of digging about the entrance; all evidence of excavation is left above the working tunnel and may be as much as thirty or forty feet from the entrance. Chipmunks are so conscious of the security of the burrow entrance that, even after long association with humans and the conviction that we are harmless, it is only in desperation at leaving new-born young unattended for too long that a female will nervously enter her burrow while being watched. Details of the burrow are in chapter 7.

Although chipmunks may be seen entering other burrows to steal food, occupancy is strictly solitary except when the female is raising young. The nesting chamber is made comfortable and warm with dry, shredded leaves carried in by mouth, not in the pouches. Droppings are not found in the burrow. Food is stored both in the nesting and storage chambers, and it is obvious that happiness to a chipmunk is a lumpy bed of acorns on which to sleep in the security of plenty.

Social Behavior. One of the most characteristic behavioral features of the chipmunk is its solitary existence. Social interaction of a relatively peaceful nature occurs only during the brief period of courtship and mating and during the six to eight weeks that the young spend with the mother after birth. At all other times, encounters between chipmunks, even between parents and their young and between siblings, result in aggressive responses. In human terms, this could be called minding your own business or looking out for yourself, and among chipmunks, the survival profit is immense.

Communication. Since chipmunks are solitary animals, one would expect to observe stereotyped communication as opposed to the graded social variety. While the details are described in chapter 5, a summary is given here of acoustic, chemical, and visual responses.

The vocal repertoire of the chipmunk consists of five more or less stereotyped sounds: the chip, the chuck, the trills, the whistle or squeal, and chatter. Chip and chuck are onomatopoetic words that accurately describe the sounds produced.

The chip is a high-pitched, birdlike sound that may be expressed once, or repeatedly, in a regular rhythm for thirty minutes or more at a rate of from 80 to 180 per minute. Because it is the loudest sound produced by the chipmunk, it is the most frequently heard and the word chipmunk may be related to it. In spite of the exuberance with which it is sometimes uttered, the chip appears to have only intrinsic communicative value, that is to say, it expresses only "I am a chipmunk, I am where I am," and possibly "I am the particular chipmunk that I am, and I am happy, sad, or annoyed." The conclusion that it has no semantic content or directed message arises from the observation that the behavior of other chipmunks is not directed by it. They do not appear to be attracted to an area in which the song is sung, nor do they appear to avoid the area, even if it is a customarily defended territory.

On the other hand, the chuck, which some consider to be nothing more than a low-pitched, soft chip, is a semantic sound that expresses anger, annoyance, caution, or outright fear. When a chipmunk hears

the chuck song, rhythmically similar to the chip song, it pays attention and, when the song follows the sighting of a hawk by the vocalist, all of the chipmunks within hearing become immobile until the song ends. Single chucks are frequently whispered as threats.

Trills consist of rapidly repeated chips or chucks of about one second duration and may or may not be semantic. The chip-trill is commonly heard when the animal is startled and scampers for cover, when it is pounced upon by another, when it pounces upon another, or simply as an expression of exuberance. The chuck-trill is usually produced by an aggressor as it attacks another. A trill of intermediate pitch frequently accompanies play or courting by the male. The high-pitched squeal is usually heard during fights, and, during mating chases, it is transformed into a whistling sound of very high pitch and long duration. Chatter, which sounds like a human voice played back at a higher speed than that at which it was recorded and is similar to the growling heard from gray squirrels, is occasionally heard during fights and during strongly directed threats. It is frequently heard between the mother and her young. In summary, the vocal repertoire, although quite rich in sounds, confirms that solitary behavior requires little in the way of semantic communication.

Chemical communication appears to be poorly developed and is confined primarily to the detection by males of females in heat (estrus). Although chipmunks may appear to mark areas by urination and defecation, other chipmunks do not seem to be influenced by these signs. Visual communication assumes a degree of importance in this solitary species, perhaps because vocalization is so limited and communication only becomes important at close range. Their characteristic markings make for easy recognition during the mating seasons and their characteristic postures must certainly be interpreted. During aggressive encounters, piloerection (hair raising) and ear and eye movement also add unmistakably to the broadcast of their attitudes and intentions.

Agonistic Behavior. Outside of the two social situations alluded to above, when two chipmunks meet, they display what appears to be a sincere dislike for one another. Three kinds of encounters, described in detail in chapter 6, are common: male territorial encounters during the mating season, territorial expulsions in any season, and encounters at feeding or food-gathering sites. A typical incident at a feeding site will generally lead to this sequence of events:

1. Frozen posture, visual fixation of 0.5 to 10 seconds' duration. If one breaks the stare, the other attacks and pursues. If one simply withdraws, the other may or may not pursue. If neither occurs—
2. Threat. The more aggressive delivers a vocal threat in the form of a single chuck or a chuck-trill, or more frequently a visual threat in the form of lowered ears, narrowed eyes, piloerection, exposed teeth, etc. If the other withdraws, it may or may not be pursued. If it does not withdraw—
3. Roll-tumble fight, complete with biting, scratching, followed by withdrawal and—
4. Chase of from three to thirty feet in distance. As the chase proceeds, the pursued naturally heads for home and the pursuer moves away from home. The former gains confidence as it approaches its territory and the latter loses confidence as the distance from its territory increases. At the territorial boundary, usually ten to fifteen feet from the burrow entrance, the roles reverse and the pursued becomes pursuer. They seldom overtake one another, but if their burrows are close together, the chase reversal may occur several times.

The territory of a chipmunk may be described as the visual distance around the burrow entrance. The classic territory, defined by William H. Burt as the area an animal will defend, is not completely recognized by the chipmunk since it spends so much of its time below ground and, therefore, is not aware of territorial intrusions. It is more appropriately the area in which it dominates all other chipmunks and can be wagered upon to win a fight. Females are generally more territorial and, therefore, appear to be more aggressive. The absence of complete territoriality is supported by the frequency with which chipmunks will enter each other's unoccupied burrows in order to steal food.

Away from the burrow, at feeding and harvesting sites, territoriality is replaced by a frequently challenged dominance order in which each chipmunk seems to know its place. Those whose burrows are within forty or so feet of the site usually dominate, but among those living more remotely, there seems to be no relationship between dominance and distance from home. Size and innate aggressiveness seem to win the day.

The most serious results of fighting are usually tail shortenings since, during the chase, teeth and tail are relatively close together. Consequently, chipmunks are often identifiable by the length of their tails and the designs of the tips after the fur has grown back in a characteristically tufted pattern.

Private Life—Annual Behavior

Hibernation. Chipmunks are seen infrequently during the winter over their entire range. They begin to disappear between early October in the Far North and early December in the Far South. Reappearance occurs in mid-March and late January respectively. The typical hibernation period in Virginia lasts from mid-November to early February. One of the most significant remaining mysteries in their life history is the when and why of hibernation. There seems to be no pattern to it. Some

Figure 81. Annual history of the Eastern chipmunk.

	Jan	Feb	Mar	Apr	May	Jun	Jul	Aug	Sep	Oct	Nov	Dec
Emergence	* * * *	* * * *										
Mating		* * *	* * *				* * *					
Parturition			* * *	* *				* * *				
Appearance of young					* * * *				* * *			
Dispersal of young					* * *	* *				* * *		
Hibernation	* * *	* * *									* * * *	* * * *

| | Jan | Feb | Mar | Apr | May | Jun | Jul | Aug | Sep | Oct | Nov | Dec |

chipmunks remain active all winter, others are not seen at all for three months, and there is no predicting which will do what from year to year. This fascinating unpredictability is discussed in chapter 2. During hibernation, laboratory studies have shown that chipmunks do not remain torpid for more than three to six days, but become active every few days during which they accomplish their normal physiological functions even if they do not leave the burrow. In this sense, it must be concluded that the adaptation to true hibernation, as exemplified in the ground hog, is not complete in the chipmunk. Nor is its survival value established, since it has been shown that winter-active chipmunks are more likely to survive than those in hibernation. In any case, their cheerful activities are missed during the late and early months of the year and their absence completes the gloom of winter.

Reproductive Behavior. The primary subject of chapter 3 is presented here in outline. Following the gloom of winter, males usually emerge from hibernation during late January through February with testicles fully descended, that is, in breeding condition. They spend their days touring the female territories on a regular basis. When they encounter one another, they engage in ritualistic wrestling matches, or tournaments, in which they fight furiously

for a few seconds without biting, break up and pose aggressively, resume wrestling. Anywhere from two to ten such jousts may occur before one retires from the field without being pursued. Should they encounter a female that is not ready to mate—and should they be foolish enough to advance their cause—they will inevitably be soundly thrashed and driven far from the area. Males generally try to mate in their first spring season, but they are often outmaneuvered by their more experienced elders.

Females begin to emerge about two weeks later in mid-February through early March and achieve estrus within a few days. They too usually mate during their first spring season at six or eleven months of age. On the day that an estrous female emerges, she may be greeted by several waiting males or by only one that has taken control of the area. In the latter case, courtship is brief, with a few trills and a bit of affectionate nudging on the part of the male, who expresses his definite intentions with rapid, vertical tail movements. At all other times chipmunks shake their tails only horizontally. Mating occupies one to two minutes, with the male thrusting rapidly while holding the female's hips with his forepaws, and with the female concentrating on remaining stationary. No sound is produced. After mating, the two may remain together for from twenty minutes to about two hours, grooming and eating, before the female drives the male away. Females appear to mate only once.

If several males are waiting for the female when she emerges, a typical mating chase results. As many as four or five males are off in determined pursuit, like little freight trains dashing through the woods. When the female needs a rest, she simply stops and then sneaks off, while her pursuers fight among themselves before realizing that she has escaped and setting off in renewed pursuit. Finally, when the strongest and presumably the smartest male is the only one left in pursuit, she selects the place for mating.

After the spring mating season, which occupies the last two weeks in February to the last two weeks in March in eastern Virginia and may be as late as the end of April in the North, the male's testicles usually retract somewhat, only to descend again in early July for the less frequent summer mating season, which, curiously, seems to occur during July throughout the range. By September, his testicles have completely retracted and he is distinguishable from a female only by close examination. The testicles of the season's young males may, if hibernation does not intervene, descend as early as December.

The female spends the thirty-one day gestation period excavating and furnishing the nest. Her diet increases in animal protein and she retires to her burrow anywhere from one week to one day before parturition, reappearing from one day to one week later. At first she is only out for brief periods, which gradually lengthen as weaning time approaches. The three to seven young are born blind, deaf, naked, and weighing about 1/6 ounce. Their teeth and fur appear gradually; the ears open in twenty-two days and the eyes in about thirty days, at which time the young are weaned. They emerge from the burrow when they are about forty days old and have attained 70 percent of their full growth. The youngsters remain close to the burrow entrance for two or three days,

attended by their mother before beginning to wander, while learning to climb, navigate, and defend themselves. The last they learn through playful encounters with siblings as they assume a pattern of dominance.

After from six to eighteen days, depending on the mother's maternal nature and tolerance, they are forbidden access to the burrow and are dispersed. This act is accompanied by general song (epideictic vocalization) in which the entire population joins and which informs the dispersing juveniles of the population density, or how far they must travel in order to find enough space in which to settle. Usually one or two females, or occasionally a male, will settle within fifty feet of the natal burrow. The others leave the area completely. During this period they are subject to persecution by the entire adult population. Some will move into unoccupied burrows or excavate their own within a few weeks. Others may be seen wandering and hiding food on the surface as late as July. These family matters are the subject of chapter 4.

The entire process may be repeated during the last two weeks in July, with parturition at the end of August and emergence in early October. Many of these late juveniles remain active all winter. Although they show a slightly lower rate of survival because they are dispersed so close to winter, they have the compensatory advantage over their spring-born relatives of knowing where the acorns are when they settle. At this point in the calendar, a chipmunk's joy is in harvesting the bounty of the oak and hickory trees until winter sets in and persuades it to retire.

Population Dynamics. The three principal requirements for any animal are food, space, and mates, and these will regulate the population in terms of the effects of territoriality, food supply, stress, and predation. Although these are not exclusive factors, we can evaluate them separately on the chipmunk's terms.

Territoriality is, of course, related to

space and implies the minimum elbow room required by an individual and the maximum number of animals that can live in an area. That maximum appears to be about twenty-five per acre when food is plentiful. In addition, the social hierarchy away from the burrow regulates population density by discouraging subordinates from remaining in the area, while it supports survival by conserving the energy that would otherwise be used in fighting. Dispersal is obviously a function of territoriality.

Food supply probably affects adults only in times of great density because of the chipmunk's ability to store virtually a lifetime supply of food in a single season. Thus, the instinctive food hoarding is one of *Tamias's* best features. Juveniles, on the other hand, must compete with their experienced elders in storing food during their first season. Those who are well endowed with the instinct will survive and continue the selection process. When a food supply fails—the acorn crop, for instance—chipmunks are more likely to hibernate, perhaps out of boredom at not having food available to harvest, and their winter survival is threatened. Assuming that both hibernation and food hoarding are genetically controlled, there would seem to be a regulatory balance implied by two competitive instincts. Possibly the strength of the food hoarding instinct has prevented the chipmunk from evolving an ability to hibernate deeply like the ground hog.

The stress of crowding results from abnormally high encounter rates, which have been shown to seriously affect the adrenal-pituitary system and may result in infrequent ovulation, abnormal young, and impaired lactation. In addition, crowding can produce interrupted matings and impaired ability to care for the young as well as selection for more aggressive genotypes that encourage dispersal.

Predation in the form of hawks, weasels, rats, snakes, cats and dogs (both wild and domestic), foxes, raccoons, and humans takes its toll and naturally increases as populations become more dense.

Large-scale population studies have shown the average lifespan of the chipmunk to be about 1.3 years and the maximum to be about 12 years. Population densities range from about two to thirty per acre.

Notes

All sources consulted in the writing of this book are listed in the Bibliography. When a reference is to one of several works by the same author, the particular citation is located below by page number and identified, when necessary, by a phrase from the text.

1. Little Chipmunk, Who Are You?
12   Black, 1963.
12   More recent evidence: Ellis and Maxson, 1979, 1980; Emry and Thorington, 1981.
14   *Eutamias* fossils . . . in Virginia: Guilday et al., 1977; *Tamias* fossils . . . in Texas: Roth, 1972.
14   Black, 1963.
14   Ellis and Maxson, 1979.

2. Lady Cheltenham and Guilford
21   Burroughs, 1916.
24   Panuska and Wade, 1957.
25   Yerger, 1953.
29   "Central Place Foraging Theory": Kramer and Nowell, 1980.
29   Burroughs, 1916.

3. Lady Cheltenham and Fenwick: The Mating Season
40   descriptions of mating behavior in the literature: Henisch and Henisch, 1970; Smith and Smith, 1975; Elliott, 1978.
40   Dunford, 1972.
45   Two seasons have been confirmed in New York: Yerger, 1955; Dunford, 1972; in Michigan: Burt, 1940; in Ohio: Condrin, 1936; in Indiana: Schooley, 1934; in Ontario: Pidduck and Falls, 1973; in Ottawa: Smith and Smith, 1975; Only one season has been reported in Wisconsin: Panuska and Wade, 1957; in Minnesota: Forbes, 1966.
45   Yerger, 1953.

4. Lady Cheltenham's Family
47   determined by dissection and counting embryos or placental scars: Smith and Smith, 1952.

48   described aspects of growth and
     development: Smith and Smith, 1972.
49   Burroughs, 1916.

5. Lady Cheltenham Alone
59   rudimentary anal scent glands:
     Yahner, 1979.
61   Burroughs, 1916.
63   the larvae . . . later emerge as adults:
     Bennett, 1955, 1972, 1973.
71   Dunford, 1970.
80   Uinta Ground Squirrel, *Spermophilus:*
     Balph and Balph, 1966; Belding's
     Ground Squirrel, *S. Beldingi:* Sherman,
     1977; California Ground Squirrel, *S.
     beecheyi:* Fitch, 1948; Western chip-
     munks, *Eutamias:* Brand, 1976; Miller,
     1944.

6. Gutrune and Hannibal: Social
Interaction
83   Dawkins, 1976.
86   game of "resident fights; intruder
     flees" is obviously a stable one: Daw-
     kins, 1976.
88   Studies have shown . . . death and
     injury can result from the inability of
     the loser to escape: Brenner et al.,
     1978; Wolfe, 1966; Dunford, 1970.
88   Yahner, 1979.

7. A Community of the
Self-Absorbed
 95   Panuska and Wade, 1956.
 95   Panuska and Wade, 1960.
100   Burroughs, 1916.
103   Yerger, 1953.
105   alterations in the endocrine or hor-
      monal system of physiological regula-
      tion: Leshner, 1978.
105   Christian and Davis, 1964.

8. The Evolution of Independence
109   Brenner and Lyle, 1975.
111   Black, 1963.

9. Summary of the Life History of
the Eastern Chipmunk
116   Panuska and Wade, 1957.

Appendixes

A

Biographies of Five Chipmunks

Lady Cheltenham

Lady Cheltenham, a small female of medium-bright color with inconspicuous eye margins, was, judging from her appearance and behavior in November, born in March 1974. During her first season her left ear became notched at its tip during a fight. By fall she had constructed a marvelously complex burrow in which she had hoarded, with paranoid intensity, what must have been a lifetime supply of white oak acorns. She remained active the entire winter of 1974–75, harvesting supplies and even stealing from other burrows.

On February 15, 1975, she mated with Fenwick. Her young were born on March 18; four emerged from the burrow on May 3 and were dispersed around May 20. Her tail was shortened by about half an inch that May in a fight and thereafter exhibited a forked tuft of fur at its tip by which she was always easily identified. During June she became tame enough to climb into my hand in order to feed, after which she became hostile during each pregnancy and period of child rearing, her tameness always returning on the day her young were to emerge. She retired into hibernation on November 22, 1975.

On February 18, 1976, eighty-seven days later, Lady Cheltenham emerged from her winter rest and on February 23 mated with Fenwick again. Six young emerged on May 4 and were dispersed on May 16. During the spring of 1976 she studied voice and developed the habit of frequently executing her "battle cry" (chiruup-chip-chip-chip), sometimes embellished with figures and trills, when she left the entrance to her burrow en route to a heavily used feeding area. No other chipmunk in this study has shared her vocal talents. Upon daily emergence, she could often be counted upon to climb a nearby tree and deliver her "morning song" for about ten minutes of chipping. She mated with Launcelot on July 17. Five

young emerged on September 28 and were dispersed on October 9. One of these was Mistress Earwicker, who refused to be completely dispersed and constructed a burrow about fifteen feet north of her mother's, and the two remained in moderately hostile family conflict. Lady Cheltenham retired into hibernation on December 5.

On February 15, 1977, seventy-one days later, she awakened. She mated on February 25, six young emerged on May 13, and were dispersed on May 19. On May 17 she appeared to be lame, running mouselike on all four feet rather than chipmunklike with a normal bounding scamper. Since close inspection revealed no injury, her condition was attributed to arthritis, probably of the hip joints or the spine. She did not seem to be seriously handicapped, however, and her condition improved over the summer until she appeared almost normal by the time she retired, without a second mating, on November 11, 1977.

Reappearing 120 days later, on March 12, 1978, she seemed to move in a normal manner. She mated on March 15, six young emerged on May 30, and were dispersed shortly after June 3. Swift dispersal was necessitated by the recurrence of her lameness, again on May 17. Her late-summer activity was inhibited by her handicap and by the persecution to which she was subjected by the other chipmunks, including her daughter, Mistress Earwicker. She improved slightly over the summer, however, and apparently was able to mate secretly during the fall with Ipswich, for at least one youngster was observed in her burrow as late as November 24 before she retired for the winter on December 15, 1978.

She emerged from hibernation seventy-four days later, on February 28, 1979, in a semicrippled state and was not seen after March 27. Mistress Earwicker moved into her burrow on May 19. Lady Cheltenham's demise could be attributed to predation, since she was quite lame at the time, or it could have resulted from her inability to maintain another pregnancy.

During the slightly more than five years of occupancy, she used no less than 30 entrances to her burrow.

Guilford

Guilford, a large, bright-colored male with conspicuous eye margins, was, judging from his behavior and appearance, probably born in August 1973 or March 1974. He established a burrow under a rotten stump and its extent seemed to indicate that he was using root tunnels, since its first two observed entrances were twelve feet apart. He may not, however, have been the first occupant.

When first observed in November 1974, he was actively harvesting acorns in un-authoritative competition with Lady Cheltenham. He retired for the winter on November 28, reappearing on January 23, 1975, through the snow and in breeding condition. After attempting to mate prematurely with Lady Cheltenham, for which he was soundly thrashed, he mated successfully on February 8 with several other females before Fenwick established his own male dominance in the area. During the second week in March Guilford was observed to have an abscessed left cheek, probably resulting from a puncture wound during a fight. He apparently succumbed to this shortly after March 21. Gutrune was using his burrow and entrance on March 24, 1975.

Gutrune

Gutrune, an extremely large female of light color with conspicuous eye margins, moved into Guilford's burrow on March 24, 1975, just before delivering a litter of young, probably on March 26. The young (three) emerged on May 4 and were dispersed on May 11. It was not possible to determine her age—she must have been at least one and probably two years old—or why she had abandoned her previous (unknown) quarters so late in gestation.

She immediately became the dominant citizen of the feeding area, ruthlessly exercising her authority on all trespassers, birds and squirrels included. She deferred for a brief time in July only to Hannibal, a supremely self-confident and gentle male from the south who used the feeding area for about two weeks, swept her off her feet, and became the one true love of her life. They mated on July 25. Three young emerged on October 4 and were dispersed on October 11 to seek their fortunes. One of these was Guinevere, who set up housekeeping about thirty feet northeast of her mother's burrow and continued to receive slightly deferential treatment from her.

During this pregnancy Gutrune became excessively obese and remained so. She was active throughout the winter of 1975–76 except for the period between January 3 and January 27, 1976.

She mated with Launcelot on February 19, 1976. Five young emerged on May 2 and were dispersed on May 12. She mated again on July 18, releasing four youngsters from the burrow on September 28 to be dispersed on October 7. During November she renovated her burrow extensively, opening a work hole through which she expelled rocks larger than herself. She retired for the winter on December 24.

On February 17, 1977, fifty-four days later, Gutrune reappeared, mated with Fenwick on February 21. Four young were observed on May 3, and were dispersed on May 14. She was not seen after August 4, when two of her most recent youngsters, Pilfer and Pillage, began systematically and competitively looting her burrow. The burrow has since remained unoccupied. The other chipmunks did not seem to mourn her passing.

Mistress Earwicker

Mistress Earwicker, a moderate-sized, brightly colored female with a median stripe extending all the way to her tail, was born on August 17, 1976, in Lady Cheltenham's burrow. As is customary with chipmunks, Launcelot, the sire, was not in attendance. Her mother's efforts at dispersal in early October were not entirely successful and Mistress Earwicker established quarters about 15 feet to the north under a group of oak trees. She retired for the winter on December 24.

Reappearing fifty-five days later, on February 19, 1977, she mated with Willoughby on February 25. Four youngsters emerged from her burrow on May 12 and were dispersed on May 19. She was the first female chipmunk observed mating at six months of age. She spent the summer and the fall persecuting her mother and entered hibernation on November 18.

On March 22, 1978, 123 days later, Mistress Earwicker reappeared, mated almost immediately with Ipswich, introduced four youngsters to the world from her burrow on May 28, dispersed them on June 3. She mated again on July 24 with Willoughby. Two or three young emerged on October 5 and were dispersed almost immediately. She continued persecuting her lame mother and retired for the winter on December 26.

In 1979 she appeared on February 3, and mated with Ipswich on February 25. Four or five young emerged on May 15, were immediately moved into Lady Cheltenham's vacant burrow, and then were dispersed on May 19, while the mother remained in the ancestral home. One of the youngsters was Clorindas, who remained in the area and is now residing in the family burrow.

On July 7, 1979, Mistress Earwicker carelessly approached her burrow entrance only to be greeted by a large domestic cat belonging to the minister down the road. Although she escaped into the burrow and was heard inside for several days, she apparently succumbed to her injuries and Clorindas took up residence on August 23. Mistress Earwicker was the only chipmunk in the community who challenged her mother's vocal talents.

Fenwick

Fenwick, a moderate-sized male, darkly colored with inconspicuous facial markings, was probably born in the spring of 1973. He appeared in the area on February 2, 1975, taking up residence in modest quarters just ten feet south of Gutrune's estate which, at the time, was still occupied by Guilford. Through industrious application of his talents he quickly became the dominant male in the neighborhood, accomplishing more matings than all of the other resident males. His first conquest was the subjugation of Guilford (possibly inflicting the wound that caused the latter's death), followed by mating with Lady Cheltenham.

Fenwick ranged far and wide during the mating season and was difficult to follow. In major encounters he lost out only to Hannibal in the summer of 1975 for the attention of Gutrune. He remained in breeding condition until the end of September and was, on one occasion, seen propositioning a juvenile. He retired for the winter on November 15. During May his tail was damaged in a fight with Lady Cheltenham so that he lost control of the tip, giving it a flaglike appearance that served to identify him at great distances.

He reappeared seventy days later on January 23, 1976, in breeding condition and increased his home range to more than an acre while keeping all of the female burrows under surveillance. He seemed to be everywhere at once, achieving a large number of successful matings during the spring and summer seasons. During October, in response to the increasing intensity of territorial conflicts with Gutrune, he moved his quarters about forty feet southeast into the woods. He retired to hibernation on November 25, reappearing sixty-six days later on January 31, 1977.

Fenwick repeated his reproductive successes, including the conquest of Gutrune and of her daughter, Guinevere, during the 1977 season, retiring on October 24. Reappearing 122 days later, on February 25, 1978, he began a similar season, from which he retired even earlier, on September 6. On March 3, 1979, Fenwick was seen active again, but the strenuous life had taken its toll and his sexual exploits were outdone by others. His flaglike tail was seen only occasionally through the 1979 season.

B

Catalog of Eastern Chipmunk Behaviors

GENERAL MAINTENANCE BEHAVIOR

Predictive Postures in Various Situations

Relaxed upright:	"Duckpin." Forepaws to breast, not clasped.
Relaxed down:	Typical resting position.
Alert seated:	Ears up, forepaws on ground.
Paw raised:	Indecision, precedes activity.
Alert upright:	Back straight. Chipping position.
Extended upright:	Back stretched, shoulders raised to extend vision.
Coiled upright:	Head lowered in direction of impending movement. (Chipping.)
Slouched down:	Back arched, paws under body. (Chipping.)
Coiled down:	Back arched, head almost on ground and extended in direction of impending movement. Chucking position. (Chipping.)
Frozen:	Body low, flattened to be inconspicuous. Sometimes back arched in aggressive encounter. Chucking position.
Exploratory:	Hind feet in place, forefeet extended toward source of curiosity. Tail moves horizontally in whiplike slow motion. Hind feet may stamp alternately.
	Frequent back jumps, soft trills.
Tail positions:	Relaxed. Loose or coiled around feet or body.
	Extended. For balance in movement.
	Alert. Straight horizontally or slightly raised.
	Upright. "Tail in air." Alarm.
	Coiled. Arched over body squirrel-like (rare).

Sleeping (Allen, 1938)
Ball-like position.
Kitten-like position.

Locomotion
Normal bounding scamper, tail horizontal (see tracks).
Walking. Feet alternately. Foraging or searching slowly.
Climbing. Hind and forefeet in unison, squirrel-like.
Jumping.
Swimming (Allaire, 1975).

Grooming (Maintenance and Displacement Behavior)

Washing:	Licking, biting, wiping with licked forepaws.
Tail grooming:	Tail is run over tongue through space between teeth.
Scratching:	With hind feet rapidly.
Shaking:	Doglike (rarely seen).
Ground grooming:	Rolling or moving under leaves, moss, roots in order to remove foreign material from fur. Dusting rare.

Comfort Movements
Defecation: Body flat, back arched, tail slightly raised.
Urination: Body flat, back arched, tail slightly raised.
                         Neither appear to be used for territorial marking.
                         Ignored by other chipmunks.
Stretching: Especially while hanging from hind feet, back arched outward, forearms freely extended outward (Ooh, that feels good!).
Sunning: Lounging about in relaxed down position.

Ingestion
Deft manipulation of food with forepaws.
Gnawing (incisors).
Chewing (molars).
Swallowing.
Drinking: Slurping with mouth submerged or licking water from leaves, etc.

Gathering and Caching Food
Foraging: Short movements with frequent periods of alertness.
                         Head never down for more than one or two seconds.
Picking up food with forepaws or mouth.
Pouch filling: Small objects picked up with mouth, deposited in pouches by mascular action or with aid of tongue. Larger objects picked up with forepaws, trimmed of sharp edges, forced into pouches with forepaws.
                         Pressure applied externally to rearrange contents.
                         Large objects sometimes expelled, repositioned, lubricated with saliva, repouched.
Hiding food: Pouch contents expelled into grass or under leaves, surface pushed down with forepaws alternately, then patted down the same way. Seen only in recently dispersed (homeless) juveniles and females with weaned young in burrow.

Digging
Scratching with forepaws either alternately or together.
Kicking with hind feet together.

Nesting
Large leaves (usually oak) picked up with mouth, folded with forepaws, forced into mouth in compact bundle. Not pouched.

SOCIAL BEHAVIOR

Reproductive
Male exploration of female territories.
Male territorial
  tournaments: Freezing and fixation, head to tail, back arched.
                         Combat. Rolling, kicking, but no biting.
                         Break and repeat.
                         Withdrawal of subordinate, no pursuit.

Guarding:	Male guards female burrow near estrus.
Mating chases:	Several males pursue female, whistles, growls.
	Female hides, slips away while males fight among themselves.
	Repeat until only one male is left in pursuit.
	Female selects mating site.
Courting:	Male tail flicks vertically.
	Nudging, nuzzling, licking.
Copulation:	Mounting.
	Intromission.
	Thrusting.

Postcopulatory grooming.

Agonistic

Freezing and fixation:	Piloerection, ears back, eyes narrowed.
Threat:	Mouth open, gesture, chuck-trill.
Rush.	
Flight:	Escape leap.
Locked mutual fighting:	Kicking, biting, scratching, growling.
Chase.	
Territorial attack:	Chip-trill, but no threat.

Contact with Nonspecifics

Alertness.
Flight.
Unconcern.
Chuck song in response to presence of predator.

Contact between Female and Young

Protective guarding, sometimes enforced with song.

Discipline:	Denial of emergence from burrow, forced incarceration in burrow.
Grooming:	Sometimes in response to nursing attempts.

Dispersal Behavior

Denial of entry to burrow.
Typical agonistic explusion from territory.

C

Taxonomic History of the Eastern Chipmunk

Genus TAMIAS Illiger
Tamias Illiger 1811. Type [*Sciurus*] *striatus* Linnaeus 1758.

Tamias striatus (Linnaeus)

[*Sciurus*] *striatus* Linnaeus 1758
Myoxus striatus, Boddaert 1784
[*Sciurus striatus*] *americanus* Gmelin 1788
Tamias americana, Kuhl 1820
Sciurus americanus, Fischer 1829
Sciurus (*Tamias*) *lysteri* Richardson 1829
Tamias striatus, Baird 1857

Currently recognized subspecies and their type localities:

Tamias striatus doorsiensis Long 1971, type from Peninsula State Park, Door Co., Wisconsin.
Tamias striatus fisheri A. H. Howell 1925, type from Merritts Corners, 3¾ mi E, 1¼ mi N Ossining, Westchester Co., New York.
Tamias striatus griseus Mearns 1891, type from Fort Snelling, Hennepin Co., Minnesota.
Tamias striatus lysteri (Richardson 1829), type from Pentanguishene, Ontario.
Tamias striatus ohionensis Bole and Moulthrop 1942, type from Cincinnati, Hamilton Co., Ohio.
Tamias striatus peninsulae Hooper 1942, type from Barnhart Lake, 3 mi SE Millersburg, Presque Isle Co., Michigan.
Tamias striatus pipilans Lowery 1943, type from 5 mi S Tunica, West Feliciana Parish, Louisiana.*
Tamias striatus quebecensis Cameron 1950, type from St. Felicien, Lake St. John Co., Quebec.
Tamias striatus rufescens Bole and Moulthrop 1942, type from Chesterland Caves, Chester Twp., Geauga Co., Ohio.
Tamias striatus striatus (Linnaeus 1758), type locality fixed by A. H. Howell as upper Savannah River, South Carolina.
Tamias striatus venustus Bangs 1896, type from Stilwell, Adair Co., Oklahoma.

---

* Jones and Suttkus (1979) equate this subspecies with *T. striatus striatus.*

D

Taxonomic Description of the Eastern Chipmunk

(Slightly modified from Howell, 1929)

Genus *TAMIAS* Illiger 1811

Generic characters—Skull relatively long and narrow; brain case slightly flattened; lambdoidal crest well developed; fronto-parietal region relatively broad; interorbital constriction narrow; postorbital processes broad at base and rather short; temporal region slightly convex (not flattened); rostrum broad at base and narrowing evenly from base to tip, its dorsal surface evenly convex (not flattened), zygomata rather weak, evenly curved and not widely expanded; notch in posterior edge of zygomatic plate of maxillary opposite pm^4 or anterior edge of m^1; palate relatively long, ending considerably behind plane of last molars; incisive foramina small and narrow; antorbital foramen large, suborbicular, piercing the zygomatic plate of the maxillary; audital bullae relatively small; upper incisors with shallow and indistinct striations or with none; upper tooth rows slightly convergent posteriorly; molars rather weak, with very low crowns, the cusps on outer border widely spaced; metaconules usually undeveloped or very small, on both upper and lower molars; last lower molar about same size as m_2; transverse enamel folds on m^1 and m^2 usually continuous (without sulcus);

dentition: $i, \frac{2}{2}; pm, \frac{2}{2}; m, \frac{6}{6} = 20.$

External characters—Form sciurine, the body rather stout; ears prominent, rounded at the summit; tail slightly more than one-third the total length, somewhat flattened, well haired but not bushy; front feet with five toes, the first rudimentary, covered with a broad, flattened nail, the others furnished with sharp recurved claws; third and fourth toes longest; nearly equal, the second and fifth shorter; palms naked with fine tubercles—three at the base of the toes and two larges ones on the posterior palm; hind feet with five toes, the three middle ones longest and nearly equal, the fifth considerably shorter and the first still shorter, but fully developed and functional; soles hairy nearly to the bases of the toes; with four tubercles on the end of the metatarsus, between the bases of the toes; cheek pouches large, opening inside the mouth anterior to the molars and extending back to the posterior base of the ears. Weight varying from 65 to 107 grams.

The baculum is a slender bone 4.5–5 millimeters in length, nearly straight, but upturned at the tip and slightly expanded into the shape of a narrow spoon or scoop, with a slight median ridge on the under surface.

Color pattern—The dorsal surface is marked by five blackish and two whitish longitudinal stripes; a median blackish stripe extends from the occiput to the posterior back or to the rump, this bordered on either side with a band of gray or tawny about twice the width of the median stripe; on either side of these dorsal bands are a pair of shorter blackish stripes with a whitish stripe between them [these extending from the shoulders to the hips].

Pelage—Of moderate length and of soft texture; the bases of the hairs are plumbeous (this color wholly concealed by the tips unless in much worn pelage) except on the ventral surface, where the hairs are unicolor to the base—white or buffy white.

Tamias striatus fisheri HOWELL 1925

Characters—Similar to *Tamias striatus striatus** but coloration paler, especially the rump, feet, and sides of head and body; dorsal area much more grayish (less ochraceous or tawny); light dorsal stripes clearer white (less shaded with ochraceous); head and underside of tail averaging paler.

Color—Summer pelage (type, August 23): top of head russet, shaded with cinnamon; facial stripes cartridge-buff; a blackish patch behind the eye; sides of face and neck with a broad, irregular stripe of russet, bordered beneath with cinnamon-buff; ears hair brown, shaded on anterior margin with mikado brown, and on posterior margin with dull buffy white; median dorsal bands smoke gray, narrowly margined on each side with hazel; median dorsal stripe, extending from point between the ears nearly to the rump, black; two outer pairs of dark stripes of same color but much shorter, light dorsal stripes creamy white; rump and hinder back hazel; thighs ochraceous-tawny; hind feet sayal brown; front feet pinkish cinnamon; sides of head and body cinnamon-buff; tail above fuscous black, overlaid with smoke gray; tail beneath, between tawny and russet, bordered with fuscous black and edged with smoke gray; underparts creamy white, washed with pale pinkish buff. *Winter pelage* (March): very similar to the summer pelage, but rump slightly paler, gray of back more prominent and underside of tail slightly paler.

Measurements—[Summarized averages] Total length, 245 mm; tail vertebrae, 91.6 mm; hind foot, 34.2 mm; ear from notch, 15.2 mm. *Skull:* greatest length, 40.1 mm; zygomatic breadth, 22 mm; cranial breadth, 16.5 mm; interorbital breadth, 9.9 mm; postorbital breadth; 11.1 mm; length of nasals, 13.5 mm. *Weight:* 90.3 g.

---

* *Tamias striatus striatus*—Size medium (for the species); colors dark, the head and rump very dark (auburn or bay); sides of body and face deep cinnamon-buff, and white dorsal stripes usually washed with buff.

E
Reproductive Events in the Lives of Four Chipmunks

Female	Mating Date	Sire	Confinement* In Date	In Day	Out Date	Out Day	Birth** Date	Litter Size	Emergence Date	Day	Dispersal Date	Days Kept
Lady Cheltenham	2-15-75	Fenwick	3-13	26	3-19	32	3-18	4	5-3	46	5-14	12
b. 3-74?	2-23-76	Fenwick	3-19	25	3-28	34	3-25	6	5-4	40	5-16	13
d. 3-79	7-18-76	Launcelot	8-15	28	8-18	31	8-18	5	9-28	41	10-8	11
	2 77		3-13		3-30			6	5-13		5-19	7
	3 78		4-9		4-19			6	5-30		6-4	6
	9-5-78	Ipswich	10-2	27	10-9	34	10-6	>1	11-20	45	11-25	5
	3-4-79	Bohort	3-27	—	—	—	—	—	—	—	—	—
Gutrune	2 75				3-26			3	5-4		5-10	7
b. 3-73?	7-25-75	Hannibal	8-21	27	9-2	39	8-25	3	10-4	40	10-14	11
d. 7-77	2-19-76	Launcelot	3-15	25	3-27	37	3-21	5	5-2	42	5-12	11
	7-18-76	#26	8-10	23	8-31	44	8-18	6	9-28	41	10-8	11
	2-21-77	Fenwick	3-20	27	3-26	33	3-24	4	5-3	40	5-14	12
Guinevere	2 76		3-14		3-22			4	4-28		5-7	10
b. 3-75	7-17-76	Kenilworth	8-4	18	8-22	36	8-17	3	9-27	41	10-8	12
d. 1–80?	2-19-77	Fenwick	3-15	24	3-27	36	3-22	4	5-1	40	5-7	7
	2-27-78	Chuzzlewit	3-23	24	4-2	34	3-30	4	5-11	42	5-30	20
	7-31-78	Willoughby	8-28	28	9-2	33	8-31	>1	10-16	46	10-23	8
	3-4-79	Bohort					4-4	>1	5-16	42	5-23	8
Mistress Earwicker	2-25-77	Willoughby	3-21	24	4-10	44	3-28	4	5-12	45	5-18	7
b. 8-76	3-17-78	Ipswich	4-12	26	4-21	35	4-17	4	5-28	41		8
d. 7-79	7-25-78	Willoughby	8-22	28	8-30	36	8-25	>1	10-5	41	6-4	
	3-4-79	Ipswich					4-4	6	5-16	42	6-15	31

*For lack of a better term and with due respect for the Victorian ethic.

**Parturition date based upon 31-day gestation period.

Selected Bibliography

References in this list that specifically address the Eastern chipmunk are of three kinds: (a) those that are cited in the text and the notes, (b) those that may not be specifically cited but are of recent publication, and (c) those that are older but of historical significance. The remainder of the older literature can be found in the bibliographies of Elsa Allen (1938), Arthur Howell (1929), and Ralph Yerger (1953, 1955).

Allaire, Pierre N. "Unusual Behavior of the Eastern Chipmunk." *Transactions of the Kentucky Academy of Science* 36 (1975): 17.

Allen, Elsa G. "The Habits and Life History of the Eastern Chipmunk." *New York State Museum Bulletin* 314, 1938.

Allen, J. A. "A Review of Some North American Ground Squirrels of the Genus *Tamias.*" *Bulletin of the American Museum of Natural History* 3 (1890):45–116.

Aniskowicz, B. T., and Vaillancourt, J. "Agonistic Interactions among Wild Eastern Chipmunks." *Canadian Journal of Zoology* 57 (1979): 683–90.

Anthony, A., Monroe, D. W., and Stere, A. "The Effect of Hibernation on Respiration and Oxidative Phosphorylation in Chipmunk Liver Homogenates." *Proceedings of the Pennsylvania Academy of Science* 40 (1967): 43–46.

Audubon, John, and Bachman, John. *The Quadrupeds of North America.* Vol. 1. Philadelphia, 1845 and 1846.

Bailey, John W. *The Mammals of Virginia.* Richmond, 1946.

Balph, D. M. and Balph, D. F. "Sound Communication of Uinta Ground Squirrels." *Journal of Mammalogy* 47 (1966): 440–50.

Balph, David F., and Stokes, Allen W. "On the Ethology of a Population of Uinta Ground Squirrels." *American Midland Naturalist* 69 (1963): 106–26.

Bennett, G. F. "Studies on *Cuterebra emasculator* Fitch 1856 and a Discussion of the Status of the Genus *Cephenymia* Ltr. 1818." *Canadian Journal of Zoology* 33 (1955): 75–98.

———. "Further Studies on the Chipmunk Warble, *Cuterebra emasculator.*" *Canadian Journal of Zoology* 50 (1972): 861–64.

———. "Some Effects of *Cuterebra emasculator* Fitch on the Blood Activity of its Host, the Eastern Chipmunk." *Journal of Wildlife Diseases* 9 (1973): 85–93.

Black, Craig C. "Review of the North American Tertiary Sciuridae." *Bulletin of the Museum of Comparative Zoology* (Harvard) 130, no. 3 (1963).

———. "Holarctic Evolution and Dispersal of Squirrels." In Dobzhansky, T., Hecht, M. K., and Steere, W. C. (editors): *Evolutionary Biology.* Vol. 6. New York: Appleton-Century-Crofts, 1972 (pp. 305–22).

Blair, W. F. "Size of Home Range and Notes on the Life History of the Woodland Deer Mouse and Eastern Chipmunk in Northern Michigan." *Journal of Mammalogy* 23 (1942): 27–36.

Blake, Barbara H. "The Effects of Kidney Structure and Annual Cycle on Water Requirements in Golden-Mantled Ground Squirrels and Chipmunks." *Comparative Biochemistry and Physiology* 58A (1977): 413–20.

Brand, Leonard R. "The Vocal Repertoire of Chipmunks (Genus *Eutamias*) in California." *Animal Behaviour* 24 (1976): 319–35.

Brenner, Fred J. "Hereditary Basis of Fat and Hibernation Cycle in the Eastern Chipmunk." *Yearbook of the American Philosophical Society,* 1972, pp. 347–49.

Brenner, Fred J., and Lyle, P. Dennis. "Effect of Previous Photoperiodic Conditions and Visual Stimulation on Food Storage and Hibernation in the Eastern Chipmunk." *American Midland Naturalist* 93 (1975): 227–34.

Brenner, Fred J., Gaetano, Charles P., Mauser, Steve W., and Belowich, David L. "Body Weight and Social Interactions as Factors in Determining Dominance in Captive Eastern Chipmunks." *Animal Behaviour* 26 (1978): 432–37.

Bryandt, M. D. "Phylogeny of Nearctic *Sciuridae.*" *American Midland Naturalist* 33 (1945): 257–390).

Burroughs, John. *Riverby.* Boston: Houghton-Mifflin, 1894.

———. *Under the Apple Trees.* Boston: Houghton-Mifflin, 1916.

Burt, William H. "Territorial Behavior and Populations of Some Small Mammals in Southern Michigan." *Miscellaneous Publication of the Museum of Zoology* (University of Michigan) 45 (1940): 1–58.

Catesby, Mark *The Natural History of Carolina, Florida, the Bahama Islands, etc.* Vol. 2, p. 75. London, 1743.

Cavalli-Sforza, Luigi L. and Feldman, Marucs W. *Cultural Transmission and Evolution: A Quantitative Approach.* Princeton, N.J.: Princeton University Press, 1981.

Christian, John J., and Davis, David E. "Endocrines, Behavior, and Population." *Science* 146 (1964): 1550–561.

Clulow, F. V., Des Marais, A., and Vaillancourt, J. "Physiological Correlations of Population Density in the Eastern Chipmunk and the White Footed Mouse." *Canadian Journal of Zoology* 47 (1969): 427–33.

Condrin, John M. "Observations on the Seasonal and Reproductive Activities of the Eastern Chipmunk." *Journal of Mammalogy* 17 (1936): 231.

Darwin, Charles. *The Expression of the Emotions in Man and Animals.* London: Murray, 1872.

Dawkins, Richard. *The Selfish Gene.* New York: Oxford University Press, 1976.

Dueser, Raymond D., and Hallett, James G. "Competition and Habitat Selection in a Forest Floor Small Mammal Fauna." *Oikos* 35 (1980): 293–97.

Dueser, Raymond D., and Shugart, H. H. "Niche Pattern in a Forest Floor Small Mammal Fauna." *Ecology* 60 (1979): 108–18.

Dunford, Christopher. "Summer Activity of Eastern Chipmunks." *Journal of Mammalogy* 53 (1972): 176–80.

———. "Behavioral Aspects of Spatial Organization in the Chipmunk, *Tamias striatus.*" *Behaviour* 36 (1970): 215–31.

Ellerman, J. R. *The Families and Genera of Living Rodents.* Vol. 1. London: British Museum (Natural History), 1940.

Elliott, Lang. "Social Behavior and Foraging Ecology of the Eastern Chipmunk in the Adirondack Mountains." *Smithsonian Contributions to Zoology* 265 (1978): 1–107.

Ellis, L. Scott, and Maxson, Linda R. "Evolution of the Chipmunk Genera *Eutamias* and *Tamias.*" *Journal of Mammalogy* 60 (1979): 331–34.

———. "Albumin Evolution within the New World Squirrels (*Sciuridae*)." *American Midland Naturalist* 104 (1980): 57–62.

Emry, Robert J., and Thorington, Richard W. Jr. "Descriptive and Comparative Osteology of the Oldest Fossil Squirrel (*Protosciurus*)." *Smithsonian Contributions to Paleobiology.* In press, 1982.

———. "The Tree Squirrel *Sciurus* as a Living Fossil." Unpublished manuscript, U. S. National Museum of Natural History, Washington, D.C., 1981.

Engels, William L. "Winter Inactivity of Some Captive Chipmunks (*Tamias striatus striatus*) at Chapel Hill, N.C." *Ecology* 32 (1951): 549–55.

Estep, Daniel Q., Canney, E. L., Cochran, C. G., and Hunter, J. L. "Components of Activity and Sleep in Two Species of Chipmunks: *Tamias striatus* and *Eutamias dorsalis.*" *Bulletin of the Psychonomics Society* 12 (1978): 341–43.

Estep, Daniel Q., Fischer, R. B., and Gore, W. T. "Effects of Enclosure Size and Complexity on the Activity and Sleep of the Eastern Chipmunk." *Behavioral Biology* 23 (1978): 249–53.

Estep, Daniel Q., and Peacock, L. J. "Effect of Food and Water Privation on General Activity of Eastern Chipmunks." *Journal of Interdisciplinary Cycle Research* 10 (1979): 57–68.

Fisher, Ronald A. *The Genetical Theory of Natural Selection.* 2d ed. New York: Dover Publications, 1958.

Fitch, H. S. "Ecology of the California Ground Squirrels on Grazing Lands." *American Midland Naturalist* 39 (1948): 513–96.

Forbes, Richard B. "Fall Accumulation of Fat in Chipmunks." *Journal of Mammalogy* 47 (1967): 715–16.

———. "Studies of the Biology of Minnesota Chipmunks." *American Midland Naturalist* 76 (1966): 290–308.

Forsyth, Douglas J., and Smith, Donald A. "Temporal Variability in the Home Ranges of Eastern Chipmunks in a Southeastern Ontario Woodlot." *American Midland Naturalist* 90 (1973): 107–17.

Frehn, John. "Mitochondrial Respiration in Mammalian Liver During Cold Exposure and Hibernation." *Transactions of the Illinois Academy of Science* 59 (1966): 432–36.

George, J. "The Delightful Delinquents." *National Wildlife* 3, no. 3 (1965): 38–41.

Ginevan, M. "Chipmunk Predation on Bank Swallows." *Wilson Bulletin* 83 (1971): 102.

Gordon, K. "Territorial Behavior and Social Dominance Among *Sciuridae.*" *Journal of Mammalogy* 17 (1936): 171–72.

Griffin, Donald R. *The Question of Animal Awareness.* New York: Rockefeller University Press, 1976.

Guilday, John E., Parmalee, Paul W., and Hamilton, Harold W. "The Clark's Cave Bone Deposit and the Late Pleistocene Paleoecology of the Central Appalachian Mountains of Virginia." *Bulletin of the Carnegie Museum of Natural History* 2 (1977): 1–87.

Hall, E. Raymond. *The Mammals of North America.* 2d ed. New York: John Wiley, 1981.

Hamilton, William J. Jr., and Whitaker, John O. Jr. *Mammals of the Eastern United States.* Ithaca: Cornell University Press, 1979.

Henisch, Bridget and Heinz. *Chipmunk Portrait.* State College, Pa.: The Carnation Press, 1970.

Hesterberg, G. A. "Chipmunk Eats Frog." *Journal of Mammalogy* 31 (1950): 350–51.

Hough, F., and Smiley, D. "Albinism in the Chipmunk *Tamias Striatus.*" *Journal of Mammalogy* 44 (1963): 577.

Howell, Arthur H. "Revision of the American Chipmunks." *North American Fauna* 52 (1929): 1–145.

Hudson, Jack W. "The Thyroid Gland and Temperature Regulation in the Prairie Vole and Chipmunk." *Comparative Biochemistry and Physiology* 65A (1980): 173–80.

Ickes, R. A. "Agonistic Behavior and the Use of Space in the Eastern Chipmunk." Ph.D. dissertation, University of Pittsburgh, 1974.

Illiger, Johann K. W. *Prodromus Systematis Mammalium et Avium.* Berlin: Salfield, 1811.

Jones, Clyde C., and Suttkus, Royal D. "The Distribution and Taxonomy of *Tamias striatus* at the Southern Limits of its Geographical Range." *Proceedings of the Biological Society of Washington* 91 (1979): 828–39.

Klugh, A. B. "Notes on the Habits of the Chipmunk *Tamias striatus lysteri.*" *Journal of Mammalogy* 4 (1923): 29–31.

Kramer, Donald L., and Nowell, William. "Central Place Foraging in the Eastern Chipmunk." *Animal Behaviour* 28 (1980): 772–78.

Kramm, K. R., and Kramm, Deborah H. "Photoperiodic Control of Circadian Rhythms in Diurnal Rodents." *International Journal of Biometeorology* 24 (1980): 65–76.

Layne, James N. "Homing Behavior of Chipmunks in Central New York." *Journal of Mammalogy* 38 (1957): 519–20.

Leshner, Alan I. *An Introduction to Behavioral Endocrinology.* New York: Oxford University Press, 1978.

Linnaeus, Carl. *Systema Natura.* Vol. 1. 1758.

Long, C. A. "A New Subspecies of Chipmunk from the Door Peninsula, Wisconsin." *Proceedings of the Biological Society of Washington* 84 (1971): 201–2.

Lorenz, Konrad. *On Aggression.* New York: Harcourt, Brace and World, 1966.

Mares, Michael A., Adams, Richard, Lacher, Thomas E. Jr., and Willig, Michael R. "Home Range Dynamics in Chipmunks (*Tamias striatus*): Responses to Experimental Manipulation of Population Density and Distribution." *Annals of the Carnegie Museum* 49 (1980): 193–201.

Mares, Michael A., Watson, Michael D., and Lacher, Thomas E. Jr. "Home Range Perturbations in *Tamias striatus*: Food Supply as a Determinant of Home Range Density." *Oecologia* (Berlin) 25 (1976): 1–12.

Maynard Smith, John. *The Theory of Evolution.* London: Penguin Books, 1975.

Miller, A. H. "Specific Differences in Call Notes of Chipmunks." *Journal of Mammalogy* 25 (1944): 87–89.

Munro, D. W., and Anthony, A. "Respiration and Oxidative Phosphorylation in Liver Tissues from Hibernating and Active Chipmunks." *Proceedings of the Pennsylvania Academy of Science* 39 (1966): 114–20.

Nadler, Charles F. "Contributions of Chromosomal Analysis to the Systematics of North American Chipmunks." *American Midland Naturalist* 72 (1964): 298–312.

Nadler, Charles F., Hoffmann, Robert S., Honacki, James H., and Pozin, Deborah. "Chromosomal Evolution in Chipmunks with Special Emphasis on A and B Karyotypes of the Subgenus *Neotamias.*" *American Midland Naturalist* 98 (1977): 343–53.

Neal, Charles M. "Energy Budget of the Eastern Chipmunk: Convective Heat Loss." *Comparative Biochemistry and Physiology* 54A (1976): 157–60.

Neal, Charles M., and Lustic, Sheldon I. "Effects of Artificial Radiation on Energetics of the Eastern Chipmunk." *Comparative Biochemistry and Physiology* 47A (1974): 277–281.

————. "Energy Budget of the Eastern Chipmunk: Artificial Radiation." *Comparative Biochemistry and Physiology* 50A (1975): 233–36.

Neff, W. H., and Anthony, A. "Seasonal Changes in the Male Reproductive Tract of the Eastern Chipmunk." *Proceedings of the Pennsylvania Academy of Science* 37 (1964): 64–70.

Neidhardt, A. P. S. "Vocal Displays of the Eastern Chipmunk *Tamias striatus fisheri.*" Master's thesis, University of Maryland, College Park, 1974.

Neumann, Richard L. "Metabolism in the Eastern Chipmunk and the Southern Flying Squirrel During the Winter and Summer." Pages 67–74 in vol. 3 of Fischer, K.C. (Editor), *Mammalian Hibernation.* Edinburgh: Oliver and Boyd, 1967.

Otto, R. A., and Estep, J. E. "The Eastern Chipmunk." *Virginia Wildlife* 38, no. 6 (1977): 4–6.

Panuska, Joseph A. "Weight Patterns and Hibernation in *Tamias striatus.*" *Journal of Mammalogy* 40 (1959): 554–66.

Panuska, Joseph A., and Wade, Nelson J. "The Burrow of *Tamias striatus.*" *Journal of Mammalogy* 37 (1956): 23–31.

————. "Field Observations on *Tamias striatus* in Wisconsin." *Journal of Mammalogy* 38 (1957): 192–96.

————. "Captive Colonies of *Tamias striatus.*" *Journal of Mammalogy* 41 (1960): 122–24.

Pidduck, Edwin R., and Falls, J. Bruce. "Reproduction and Emergence of Juveniles in *Tamias striatus* at Two Localities in Ontario, Canada." *Journal of Mammalogy* 54 (1973): 693–707.

Pivorun, Edward B. "A Gradient Calorimeter Study of Normothermic and Hibernating Eastern Chipmunks." *Comparative Biochemistry and Physiology* 54A (1976a): 259–61.

———. "A Biotelemetry Study of the Thermoregulatory Patterns of *Tamias striatus* and *Eutamias minimus* During Hibernation." *Comparative Biochemistry and Physiology* 53A (1976b): 265–71.

———. "Hibernation of a Southern Subspecies of *Tamias striatus*: Thermoregulatory Patterns." *American Midland Naturalist* 98 (1977): 495–99.

Richter, Curt P. "Evidence for Existence of a Yearly Clock in Surgically and Self-blinded Chipmunks." *Proceedings of the National Academy of Sciences of the U.S.A.* 75 (1978): 3517–521.

Roberts, E. F., and Snyder, D. P. "Use of ^{125}I for Identifying Mother-Offspring Relationships in the Eastern Chipmunk." *Proceedings of the Third National Symposium on Radioecology.* Pages 274–81. Springfield, Va., National Technical Information Service, 1974.

Roth, Edward L. "Late Pleistocene Mammals from Klein Cave, Kerr County, Texas." *Texas Journal of Science* 24 (1972): 75–84.

Ryan, D. A., and Larson, J. S. "Chipmunks in Residential Environments." *Urban Ecology* 2 (1976): 173–78.

Schooley, J. P. "A Summer Breeding Season in the Eastern Chipmunk." *Journal of Mammalogy* 15 (1934): 194.

Scott, Grace W., and Fisher, Kenneth C. "Hibernation of Eastern Chipmunks Maintained Under Controlled Conditions." *Canadian Journal of Zoology* 50 (1972): 95–105.

Seidel, D. R. "Some Aspects of the Biology of the Eastern Chipmunk." Ph.D. dissertation, Cornell University, Ithaca, 1960.

Seton, Ernest Thompson. *Lives of Game Animals.* Vol. 4, pp. 170–215. Garden City, N.Y.: Doubleday, Doran and Company, 1928.

Sherman, Paul W. "Nepotism and the Evolution of Alarm Calls." *Science* 197 (1977): 1246–253.

Slobodkin, Lawrence B. *Growth and Regulation of Animal Populations.* 2d ed. New York: Dover Publications, 1980.

Slobodkin, Lawrence B., and Rapoport, Anatol. "An Optimal Strategy of Evolution." *Quarterly Reviews of Biology* 49 (1974): 181–200.

Smith, Donald A., and Smith, Lorraine C. "Aberrent Coloration in Canadian Eastern Chipmunks." *Canadian Field Naturalist* 86 (1972): 253–57.

———. "Oestrus, Copulation, and Related Aspects of Reproduction in Female Eastern Chipmunks." *Canadian Journal of Zoology* 53 (1975): 756–67.

Smith, Lorraine C., and Smith, Donald A. "Reproductive Biology, Breeding Seasons, and Growth of Eastern Chipmunks in Canada." *Canadian Journal of Zoology* 50 (1972): 1069–85.

Snyder, D. P. "Biology of the Eastern Chipmunk." Technical Progress Report, U.S. Atomic Energy Commission Report NYO 3626-7, 1970.

Stegman, L. C. "A Melanistic Chipmunk." *Journal of Mammalogy* 41 (1960): 514–15.

Stevenson, Henry M. "Occurrence and Habits of the Eastern Chipmunk in Florida." *Journal of Mammalogy* 43 (1962): 110–11.

Svendsen, Gerald E., and Yahner, Richard H. "Habitat Preference and Utilization by the Eastern Chipmunk." *Kirtlandia*, no. 31 (1979): 1–14.

Thomas, Kim R. "Burrow Systems of the Eastern Chipmunk (*Tamias striatus pipilans* Lowery) in Louisiana." *Journal of Mammalogy* 55 (1974): 454–59.

Thompson, J. N., Jr. "Chromosomes of Oklahoma Mammals: I. Three Species of Squirrels." *Proceedings of the Oklahoma Academy of Science* 51 (1971): 79–80.

Tryon, C. A., and Snyder, D. P. "Biology of the Eastern Chipmunk: Life Tables, Age Distributions, and Trends in Population Numbers." *Journal of Mammalogy* 54 (1973): 145–68.

Vincent, G. P., Pare, W. P., Isom, K. E., and Reeves, J. M. "Activity-stress Gastric Lesions in the Chipmunk *Tamias striatus.*" *Physiological Psychology* 5 (1977); 449–52.

Wang, Lawrence C. H., and Hudson, Jack W. "Temperature Regulation in Normothermic and Hibernating Eastern Chipmunks." *Comparative Biochemistry and Physiology* 38A (1971): 59–90.

Ward, I. L. "Prenatal Stress Feminizes and Demasculinizes the Behavior of Males." *Science* 175 (1972): 82–84.

White, John A. "Genera and Subgenera of Chipmunks." *Publication of the University of Kansas Museum of Natural History* 5 (1953): 543–61.

Wilson, Edward O. *Sociobiology.* Cambridge, Mass.: Harvard University Press, 1975.

Wolfe, James L. "A Study of the Behavior of the Eastern Chipmunk." Ph.D. dissertation, Cornell University, Ithaca, N.Y., 1966a.

———. "Agonistic Behavior and Dominance Relationships of the Eastern Chipmunk." *American Midland Naturalist* 76 (1966b): 190–200.

———. "Observations on Alertness and Exploratory Behavior in the Eastern Chipmunk." *American Midland Naturalist* 81 (1969): 249–53.

Woodward, Alvalyn E., and Condrin, John M. "Physiological Studies on Hibernation in the Chipmunk." *Physiological Zoology* 18 (1945): 162–67.

Wrazen, John A. "Late Summer Activity Changes in Populations of Eastern Chipmunks." *Canadian Field Naturalist* 94 (1980): 305–10.

Wrazen, John A., and Svendsen, Gerald E. "Feeding Ecology of a Population of Eastern Chipmunks in Southeast Ohio." *American Midland Naturalist* 100 (1978): 190–201.

Wynne-Edwards, V. C. *Animal Dispersion in Relation to Social Behavior.* Edinburgh: Oliver and Boyd, 1962.

Yahner, Richard A. "Adaptive Significance of Scatter Hoarding in the Eastern Chipmunk." *Ohio Journal of Science* 75 (1975): 176–77.

———. "Activity Lull in *Tamias striatus* During the Summer in Southeast Ohio." *Ohio Journal of Science* 77 (1977): 143–45.

———. "Seasonal Rates of Vocalization in Eastern Chipmunks." *Ohio Journal of Science* 78 (1978a): 301–3.

———. "The Sequential Organization of Behavior in *Tamias striatus.*" *Behavioral Biology* 24 (1978b): 229–43.

———. "The Adaptive Nature of the Social System and Behavior in the Eastern Chipmunk." *Behavioral Ecology and Sociobiology* 3 (1978c): 397–427.

———. "Burrow System and Home Range Use by Eastern Chipmunks: Ecological and Behavioral Considerations." *Journal of Mammalogy* 59 (1978d): 324–29.

Yahner, Richard A., Allen, B. L., and Peterson, Wesley J. "Dorsal and Anal Glands in the Eastern Chipmunk." *Ohio Journal of Science* 79 (1979): 40–43.

Yerger, Ralph W. "Home Range, Territoriality, and Populations of the Chipmunk in Central New York." *Journal of Mammalogy* 34 (1953): 448–58.

———. "Life History Notes on the Eastern Chipmunk *Tamias striatus lysteri* Richardson in Central New York." *American Midland Naturalist* 53 (1955): 312–23.

Zinn, D. J. "Albino Chipmunks in Rhode Island." *Journal of Mammalogy* 35 (1954): 585–86.

Index

This book was designed by Elizabeth Sur, typeset by Service Composition Company, Baltimore, Maryland, and printed by Kingsport Press, Kingsport, Tennessee. It was produced by the Smithsonian Institution Press, Washington, D.C.